Susan Bastone has been an avid reader and writer all her life. She spent most of her childhood gazing out of windows or with her head in a book. A love of history led her to research her family and the local and social history of her times, and a lifetime of writing: journals, poetry, articles and blogs, inspired her to write her own story.

As a school librarian, she passed on her passion for reading and writing to generations of children and has been instrumental in setting up literacy projects and awards for young people. She lives in Wiltshire with her husband, two cats and an awful lot of books.

For my children and grandchildren
With love always.
I hope I succeeded.

Susan Bastone

CORONATION BABY

A Memoir (1953 – 1973)

AUSTIN MACAULEY PUBLISHERS™
LONDON • CAMBRIDGE • NEW YORK • SHARJAH

Copyright © Susan Bastone 2022

The right of Susan Bastone to be identified as author of this work has been asserted by the author in accordance with sections 77 and 78 of the Copyright, Designs and Patents Act 1988.

All rights reserved. No part of this publication may be reproduced, stored in a retrieval system, or transmitted in any form or by any means, electronic, mechanical, photocopying, recording, or otherwise, without the prior permission of the publishers.

Any person who commits any unauthorized act in relation to this publication may be liable to criminal prosecution and civil claims for damages.

All of the events in this memoir are true to the best of author's memory. The views expressed in this memoir are solely those of the author.

A CIP catalogue record for this title is available from the British Library.

ISBN 9781398454682 (Paperback)
ISBN 9781398454699 (ePub e-book)

www.austinmacauley.com

First Published 2022
Austin Macauley Publishers Ltd®
1 Canada Square
Canary Wharf
London
E14 5AA

I would like to thank all the following people, without whom this book would not have been written.

First and foremost, to my husband of nearly 50 years, my lover, best friend and reading partner, Matthew has been my rock always.

To my sisters, who are guiltless in this story. Thank you for the love you have always shown.

To my children who have provided me with much joy, pride, fun and laughter and who have become wonderful human beings of whom I am very proud.

To my grandchildren who give me so much joy and for whom I wrote this memoir.

To my cousin Lindy, who was and still is like a sister.

To all my friends, past and present, who have shared bad times and good and always been there for me.

To the Guardian Masterclass that set me on the path to writing this memoir.

And finally, to my publisher, Austin Macauley for believing it was worth publishing.

Table of Contents

Introduction	11
Chapter One: Never Had It So Good	13
Chapter Two: World at War	30
Chapter Three: A Saxon Town	41
Chapter Four: High Days and Holidays	53
Chapter Five: Wonderland and Other Magical Worlds – Escapes into Reading	66
Chapter Six: Hopscotch, Hockey & Homer	76
Chapter Seven: The Good Life	93
Chapter Eight: Playtime	107
Chapter Nine: I Heard It Through the Grapevine	117
Chapter Ten: A Working Girl	128
Chapter Eleven: She's Leaving Home, Bye Bye	137
Chapter Twelve: A Changing World	143

Introduction

I was born Susan Caroline Pegg (known as Susie) on 28th August 1953, two months after the coronation of the young Queen Elizabeth II. My parents, Graham Ewart Pegg and Eileen Joyce, nee Stillwell, were of the immediate post war generation who had lived through the war but been too young to suffer overmuch. My mother had a 'good war', enjoying meeting a wide range of people with the influx of troops stationed along the south coast of England. My father undertook National Service in 1946 and, being a musician, was sent out to India to play for the troops, an adventure he enjoyed very much.

The reality of marriage, parenthood and keeping food on the table was probably a shock to them both. Having met at Butterworth's the publishers in the centre of London where they both worked as clerks, they were used to a good social life and, for my father at least, the trappings of the middle-class. My father had no qualifications, having left school at 14 with rheumatic fever and never returned. His parents were relatively well-off, my grandfather was a successful civil servant and his mother allowed him to spend his time on his passion for jazz rather than worry about his future.

Despite that, they had much in common with many young people of the time. Hope for the future and pride in Great Britain. Winston Churchill was once again Prime Minister and the new Welfare State promised a fairer future for everyone.

The next two decades saw rapid and prodigious change, around the world but in Great Britain in particular. The world in 1973 was very different to that of 1953. For those born at this time, there was great opportunity and I have tried to reflect the changing society I was growing up in.

I have also tried to be honest and fair about the people I shared the first twenty years of my life with. It is inevitable that I mainly see my own side of the story though, as I have grown older, I have become more sympathetic and understanding of my mother's side. Having my own children helped me to understand the challenges of parenthood. Although, at first, she tried to tell me how to bring up my children, our relationship slowly began to improve. Sadly, my mother died in 1986 before we could rebuild it completely.

Susie, aged 3 months

Chapter One
Never Had It So Good

Memory is like a friend. The more attention you pay to it, the more it gives you. Pictures appear in my head, almost unbidden.

The air is thick with black smoke though the sun is shining above it. It is Monday. Mothers rush to get the washing from the line before it is too late. It has taken hours to heat the copper, wash, rinse and mangle the clothes and no-one has the energy, or will, to do it all again tomorrow. For my mother, it will probably mean the recurrence of bronchitis and the lighting of the Wright's Coal Tar burner. She has no choice but to take to her bed and I will make her bread and dripping later for tea. The cause of her distress is Kingston Power Station, a coal-fired generating station just across the road from our house in King's Road. It has two tall chimneys, the second of which was built just five years before I was born. Every winter, there are thick fogs which stretch for miles and we can barely see the glow of the streetlights on our walk home from school or the shops. It is just as well that our National Health doctor, Doctor Lake, has a surgery in his house at the top of our road, on the corner of the busy

Richmond Road through the town. Until a few years ago, he was a private doctor and not many people like us could afford to pay. We go regularly to Doctor Lake to receive our vaccinations against many of the childhood illnesses that blight children's lives: diphtheria, tetanus, whooping cough, smallpox and, most important of all, polio. He seems old to me, but is very kind with a twinkly smile and I love his waiting room with lots of comics. Even before I can read, I love the pictures.

Kingston Power Station from the other side of the River Thames

∞

This was our life in the mid-1950s. Compared to the 21st century, it was basic, but the post-war world was full of hope and expectation: a new National Health Service, free secondary education for every child and the belief that we were entering a new golden age with a beautiful young queen on the throne, only a couple of years older than my mother and crowned just two months before I was born. The television set in our house was bought for the coronation and brought the wider world into our house as I was growing up. Grainy images of events such as Suez, the assassination of President Kennedy, England winning the World Cup and the first landing on the moon, were avidly watched and much discussed by my parents. Politics was ever present, I grew up hearing passionate arguments about the way Britain should act and how it was seen in the world. Their politics were very different. Mum grew up in a working-class household on the South Coast and was staunchly Labour. Dad, a middle class, rather spoilt young man from a privileged background, was equally firmly Conservative. It made for fireworks on many occasions.

∞

Our house was the ground floor of a spacious Edwardian semi-detached with a bay window at the front and a huge, wild garden at the back. Across the road a tree-lined avenue led down to the river and Canbury Gardens but no one in our street could ignore the looming shadow of the power station. Despite its proximity, it was, sadly, the Wright's Coal Tar burner lit to help her bronchitis, that contributed to my mother's cancer years later, rather than the smoke from the power station. I didn't know then, of course, but the house was rented and my mother's ambition was to own their own house and get away from the smoke.

Mum came from a hard-working, strict, working-class family in Sussex. The youngest of four, she was the only child to break away and go to London to seek her fortune. Living in a hostel in Chelsea and working at the publishers,

Butterworth & Co. my mother met the two most important people in her life. Sheila Wenlock became her best friend and my godmother. At the office, a young clerk and aspiring jazz musician named Graham (Gray) Pegg swept her off her feet and became my father. She was always torn between the two sides of her character: she was proud of being working class but wanted to get away from it; she loved life but felt guilty enjoying herself. Her mother, Granny Stillwell, had a core of steel and, though diminutive at only 5'2", ruled her family including our easy-going grandad, with a rod of iron. My mother inherited that and many of her mother's sayings and believed in 'spare the rod and spoil the child'. I felt the back of her hand more times than I can remember. "Stand still so I can hit you" was a common refrain. She shared that steel with her sister Joan and my cousin, Lindy, and I frequently bemoaned our strict mothers, though I think secretly we each thought the other's was easier.

Grandad and Granny Stillwell Circa 1960 *Mum and Dad on their Wedding Day 28th March 1952* *Grandad, Nana Pegg and Dad mid 1950s.*

My father was the only, and quite spoilt, child of a very middle-class family. Grandad Pegg was a World War One war hero and had worked for Winston Churchill during World War Two. Nana, my grandmother, was a socialite, enjoying the good life, who would do anything for 'her darling boy'. His strawberry birthmark had determined her never to have another child and all her love and energy went into giving him anything he wanted. When she thought she might lose him at the age of 14 due to rheumatic fever, she would not let him return to school but, instead, encouraged him to indulge his passion for jazz.

Britain looked forward and was proud of itself. 1953 was a breakthrough year in terms of moving away from austerity and towards improved living standards and a measure of affluence although the standard rate of income tax was nine shillings in the pound (45%)and butter, cheese, meat and eggs were still rationed. Great Britain was still a very class-conscious society. There might be a new young queen on the throne but Winston Churchill was, once again, Prime Minister and the British people were on the whole deferential. My fearless, intelligent, mother was swept off her feet by our charming, but rather aimless, father and was determined they were going to go up in the world. Eleven years later, when they had finally saved enough to buy their own house, she was so proud but my heart broke. I felt my life was ending. All my friends at school and Sunday School would be left behind and as a child of 10 I did not understand why. My tantrum was the beginning of a war of attrition with my mother. We left in my last year of primary school and after that, I no longer felt a child.

As a coronation baby I have seen Britain change from one of hope and expectation of the post war years, a country seemingly at ease with itself, to a nation split down the middle and unsure of its place in the world. From an era of opportunity for all and a decent society to the narrow, bleaker reality of a widening gap between rich and poor, not just financially but of opportunity too.

∞

But I'm jumping ahead of myself. There are still years of childhood and happiness to come in that house.

Auntie Jean lived upstairs. Of course, she wasn't our auntie but every female adult who wasn't a relative had to be called 'Auntie' as a mark of respect. Respectability was very important, particularly to the new, lower middle classes, who aspired to better themselves. My mother was not the only one who did the housework in the morning, cooked the lunch and then insisted we have a rest, after which she washed, put on make-up and out we went, along the main road to the town, with me holding on to the big silver cross pram, stopping every few yards for neighbours to admire the new babies – two for the price of the one she thought she was expecting! No scans in those days.

"Oh, twins, how wonderful", "Aren't they adorable!"

I wasn't sure what all the fuss was about. To me they looked like rabbits. The twins, as they were known until, understandably, they objected and insisted on being individuals, were very tiny, having weighed less at birth together than the average baby. They were born in our parents' bedroom, home births were not unusual in those days, and then taken into hospital incubators: green, metal boxes which I thought were rabbit hutches. They were named after our grandmothers: Alison (Ali) after Mum's mum, Alice Stillwell, and Darrell (Dazzy) after Dad's mum Edith, who for some reason we never found out, was nicknamed Darrell. Looking after two babies at once can never be easy but in the strictly traditional household we were, it was not a man's job to help with housework or childcare. Once they were weaned, the two baby chairs sat on top of the bath in the kitchen, mum with a spoon in each hand. I was roped in to help, though I am not sure I was ever very keen. This was the shape of things to come.

Looking back, it was probably quite a dark house and difficult to clean. It certainly had none of the modern conveniences many people already had. The rooms were one behind the other from front to back with a narrow hallway connecting them. Mum's piano was against the wall, hardly ever played. At the front was my parents' bedroom, a large bright room with tall, oak wardrobes and a cosy armchair in the corner – this is where the first photograph of the twins would be taken. A small truckle bed seemed to be a semi-permanent addition to the room; through illness or accident I slept in there many times. There were times after my sisters were born when I relished the excuse to move rooms and if I had to sleep there to stop my sisters catching mumps then I didn't mind the awful pain so much. Childhood illnesses were very common, I can still feel the daytime darkness of a room with the curtains pulled. I had measles and letting the light in would apparently make you go blind. Illness meant staying in bed, eating bland food and being very bored. There was no daytime and very little children's television to help the hours go by. There was one memorable programme however. *Watch with Mother* began on 21st April 1953 and the images are still etched into my memory: Monday was *Picture Box* with its kaleidoscope of adventure, though as it was in black and white it was not very interesting; Tuesday gave us *Andy Pandy*, a favourite doll in a blue and white striped playsuit; Wednesday was the turn of *Rag, Tag and Bobtail*, a story of three rabbits which I thought rather childish; on Thursday, it was my favourite, *The Flowerpot Men* with Bill, Ben and Little Weed; and on Friday *The Woodentops* – a family resembling Playmobil characters. Many years later, watching *Candlewick Green* and *Trumpton* with my own children brought it all back.

Our house was long and narrow with an outhouse at the back leading to a large back garden. Its rough lawn was separated from a large overgrown 'jungle' by a grassy hump which the boys next door and I used to hurtle over in our competitive games. Major, our large tabby cat, loved to race with us. I was often covered in scratches and bruises so when, one sunny afternoon, I began screaming and running up the garden, my mother in the kitchen called "What have you done now?" exasperatedly. The sight of blood pouring from my wrist, a deep cut that turned out to be extremely near the artery, must have been one of the biggest shocks of her life. My memory is hazy but I remember going in an ambulance, being fed Maltesers by a lovely black nurse (still a novelty in those days) and the pain of it afterwards when I came home with my arm in a sling. I had tripped over the grassy hump and fallen onto a broken milk bottle and bear the scar to this day. Despite the pain and discomfort, I think secretly I delighted in the attention and the drama.

The Thompson boys were my playmates. From a very young age, children played out in the street. The roads were much quieter and safer. Not many people owned cars, our dad went to work on a motor-cycle and I was allowed out on my tricycle even before I went to school. The biggest hazard was avoiding the steaming manure left by the horses of the rag and bone man's cart. Mum would often be first to collect it on a shovel 'for the roses'. There was not much traffic but I remember the steam roller laying tarmac along the main road, seemingly quite regularly. The boys were not actually next door, but next door but one. In between our long gardens was an empty house with a wilderness, a forbidden, but often visited adventure playground. Looking back, I realise it had bomb damage and was uninhabitable but we were convinced the house was haunted and dared each other to shout through the letter box at the ghosts.

Susie with twins 1958

Susie in the garden of 6 Kings Road, 1961

My room was next to my parents'. It was a large, sunny room with French windows out to the garden and lots of space for playing. Once they were old enough, my sisters were pressured into being whatever was needed in my latest game. A gap of nearly five years though did not make for easy playmates and I was content in my own company even at quite a young age. Dad was a great playmate when he was around and took pity on me when the twins were born. I was the boy he never had and certainly I had no time for dolls or other girly toys. He often got into trouble with Mum for playing instead of helping out. Dad's confinement to bed with a broken ankle when I was eight years old was an excuse for afternoons after school learning to play cribbage and keeping out of Mum's way.

The main living room of our house was crowded with furniture: a dining table, easy chairs, a dresser for our crockery, a fireplace of course and, in the very corner of the small, but cheerful room, a television. Behind the living room was the kitchen: a cooker, a refrigerator and the bath covered with a worktop. The 'fridge' was the height of affluence in the 1950s though we still shopped nearly every day so it wasn't really necessary. The tiny freezer compartment was the most exciting with its frozen peas and fish fingers and, very occasionally as a real treat, Walls ice cream in a block. There was no washing machine. Clothes were washed by hand in a copper bath and wrung outside through the mangle, a weekly drudge which was bad enough on sunny and windy days when the clothes could be pegged out to dry on the washing line but even worse in bad weather. The smell of Sunlight soap and wet clothes permeated the house. At least we did not have them hanging everywhere, our outhouse with the copper, our bikes and the toilet, held racks of drying clothes for much of the year. The one exception to this drudgery was our sheets which went to the Sunlight laundry, arriving back at the door crisp and starched, wrapped in brown paper and tied up with string. There was no easy-care linen then.

The twins' high-chairs sat on the bath worktop and were moved on Saturdays for bath night. The water was heated in the copper, the kitchen filled with steam and the long process of bathing and hair washing began. I loved it and hated it at the same time. The horrid taste of bitter aloes was a result of biting my nails to avoid them being cut. But, oh the joy of sitting in front of the fire with Mum brushing my hair until it dried, there were no hand-held hairdryers. Winceyette pyjamas and warm, fluffy dressing gowns were essential for once outside the cosy living room, the house was unheated. In winter, ice formed on the inside of our bedroom windows and getting dressed under the covers on cold winter mornings was normal. It wasn't easy, the heavy blankets and quilted eiderdown weighing me down as I struggled with a woollen vest, pants and socks, stiff from drying on the washing line.

Saturdays were good days. Dad worked as a representative (a rep) for Charringtons Coal Merchants, collecting money weekly from housewives whose only source of heating was coal. He worked on Saturday mornings and on his way home would pick up fish and chips for lunch for us all. Although this was a cheap meal in those days, it was a real treat and obviously gave Mum a day off from cooking not only lunch, but Dad's dinner in the evening too. Most days she had to cook two meals. He liked to relax in the afternoon as he would be out in the evening, playing jazz at Working Men's Clubs far and wide. His huge double bass sat proudly in my parents' bedroom. If I was lucky, he would play games: in the garden in summer and board games in winter, before leaving us all to bath time and the treat of Saturday night television: Doctor Who and Dixon of Dock Green. Subtitled *'The stories of a London policeman on his beat'*, P.C. Dixon, played by actor Jack Warner, epitomised our familiar 'bobby' as the local policeman was known. As children, we were taught that we could always trust a policeman and the dark blue uniforms and police boxes (subsequently, of course, known as *The Tardis* in Doctor Who*)*, were reassuring presences. Doctor Who, first broadcast in 1963 was a firm favourite, running weekly until 1989, followed by a 16 year gap until its re-emergence in 2005.

Sundays were not so good. Dad would have a lie in, he'd been out playing jazz late the night before. We might see him for a couple of hours before he went to the pub for a few pints before lunch. Then home for his Sunday roast and a nice snooze in the afternoon. It was not much of a life for a mother with three small children, left alone in the evenings and most of the day too. Many a plate was thrown during arguments because Mum wanted him to take us all out in the afternoon, she didn't learn to drive until the 1970s. And yet, by Sunday evening all was forgiven in the weekly get-together with their friends, playing cards at our house or down the pub. Our parents were very sociable and Mum became a different person then. Pete and Doreen, Johnny and Marge were like aunties and uncles to us and were our extended family. The men were also musicians so Sunday nights was their way of making it up to their wives who had been at home Friday and Saturday nights. I loved it when they went out. Our two lovely teenage babysitters let me stay up to watch 'Sunday night at the London Palladium' on the tiny, black and white, television. Hosted by the time I was watching it by a young and cheeky Bruce Forsyth, it was glitter and glamour the like of which we were desperate for.

In 1950s Britain, families like ours had dinner in the middle of the day. Post war food was wholesome but bland. Meat and two veg was the staple meal for everyone. Meat would be bought, though not every day, from the butcher and the cheapest cuts stewed with carrots and onions to make it go further. Every bit of fat and gristle had to be eaten. "Waste not, want not" was the mantra and I was regularly reminded of the poor starving children in Africa who would be grateful for my food – "they can have it!" I would say, risking a smart slap for my cheek. Mum was a good, plain cook and we never went hungry although if you didn't eat what was on your plate there was nothing else and you were liable to get it served up for tea. We loved toad-in-the-hole, spam fritters, and more or less anything with baked beans. Once the twins were at school, Mum's job as a book-keeper for the meat market in Kingston meant a free leg of New Zealand lamb every weekend. Although it was so far away, New Zealand had been a colony and the trade links with Great Britain meant lamb was affordable for most families. Even so, to be given one free was a real perk. Joy for her, purgatory for me. Roasted on Sunday, cold on Monday, minced up for cottage pie on Tuesday and served up for your tea if you'd left it at dinner, I learnt to loathe lamb. Sadly, even today the smell of lamb or mint sauce turns my stomach. Pudding might be fruit from a tin: pears, mandarins or fruit salad, perhaps with some Carnation milk for a treat. The only fresh fruit we ate was apples, some from the garden but also from the wonderful fruit and vegetable market in the town. When there was time, a steaming hot rice pudding was a favourite.

Dinner in the week was eaten at school of course, though at infants' school we still came home for our dinner. Tea was eaten about 4 o'clock and was the best time of the day. Never fancy but lots of toast or crumpets, dripping with butter and topped with strawberry jam, Dairylea cheese or even both together. Butter was no longer rationed and was delicious, much nicer than the new, cheaper, margarine that we started eating soon after. We might have marmite on our toast and baked beans or boiled eggs with soldiers, but whatever we were eating, Mum, me and my sisters all sat round the table and talked. There was a lot of talking in our house and teatimes were full of laughter. Friday was kippers from the market, full of bones but their lovely salty, buttery taste still evokes the promise of the weekend to come. On Sunday, we had 'high tea', ham salad or perhaps tinned salmon with round lettuce, cucumber and ripe, juicy, tomatoes in the summer. No salad in the winter of course, only what was 'in season' was available.

There were special meals too. Summer was a good time when tea might be in the garden, or a picnic by the river: Dairylea sandwiches with white sliced bread, tomatoes, boiled eggs and, joy of joys, potato crisps: little bags of plain crisps with a twisted blue paper full of salt to shake on them. There were biscuits or cakes, usually a chocolate Penguin or chocolate marshmallow. My birthday teas were the most special of all. If I close my eyes, I can see the table spread awaiting my friends. Cheese boats made with little bridge rolls, cocktail sticks and Kraft cheese slices for the sail, dainty ham sandwiches, Twiglets, glistening little sausages, jelly, ice cream and, of course, the Cake – a towering iced confection with candles on the top. A special party dress, made by my Nana, completed the picture and I would be a princess for the day.

The nation's princesses were loved by us all and there was much excitement at the wedding of Princess Margaret. I was too young to have been aware of the scandals surrounding her and her wish to marry Group Captain Peter Townsend but her marriage to a court photographer, Anthony Armstrong-Jones was a great occasion for the nation and was featured in all the newspapers. Better for me though was the 7th birthday present from my Auntie Rose of *Princess Margaret's Wedding Book*, a riot of colour in an otherwise black and white world of newspapers and television. It was to be a lasting reminder of that gentle, kindly aunt. Struck down prematurely at the age of 41, the news coming to our house via a telegram, my mother told me with tears streaming down her face. Her much-loved eldest sister left two young boys, my cousins Richard and Andrew to be brought up by their father and our mutual grandmother.

∞

Starting school was my first real taste of independence. With two small babies at home, I was very soon allowed to walk the ten minutes from home to school on my own. There were no roads to cross but the long, main road had a very strange feature. A continuous brick wall lined the pavement for two or three hundred yards and, at regular intervals, sternly closed front doors like entrances into a forbidden world. The walls were perhaps twenty feet high but there was nothing beyond them but sky. My vivid, childish imagination was both fascinated and terrified of what might lie behind those doors. There was nothing of course, just another bomb site but it was not until I travelled on the top deck of a bus, years later that the puzzle was solved.

My home and the road where I lived was the centre of my universe: across the road to the river path, up and across the main road to Richmond Park where I saw my first deer, right at the top of the road to school and left to head out towards Richmond and, more importantly, to Harrington's sweet shop. Sweet rationing ended in 1953 so our weekly trip to Harrington's meant agonies of indecision before spending our 3d (26p in today's money) on Sherbert dabs, blackjacks & fruit salads (4 for an old penny), gobstoppers or perhaps a bag of pear drops or cough candy. I would travel this road to the grammar school years later but then it felt like heading out of town. Along the wide road were large houses with long drives and large gardens, and quiet streets running down to the river. Despite the Kingstonian F.C. football ground and the Hawker Siddeley Aircraft Factory, this end of town was more rural and genteel, leading as it did to Richmond and Ham, the homes of royal palaces. Indeed, Queen Elizabeth II travelled slowly along this road in March 1961 while we children waved our flags and cheered.

∞

I am ten years old and half way into my last year at primary school. I will soon take my Eleven Plus which will determine the rest of my life. But none of that seems important. I am in despair. We are moving house and my familiar world is ending. Mum finds walking harder each winter, her bronchial chest ageing her prematurely. The trolley buses regularly take her into town to do the shopping but getting anywhere else must be done on foot. Even short walks down to the river tire her out and I go more often on my own, dreaming and wondering where the next part of my life will take me. Perhaps moving away from the power station will improve her health and our lives. This feels like the end of childhood, and perhaps it is.

Notes:

1 Family Britain, David Kynaston
2 UK Finance Act 1953
3 Watch with Mother, BBC TV programme for children 1950s.

Chapter Two
World at War

Tears are streaming down my father's face. I am frightened, I have never seen him cry before. *"Oh my God, there will be another war,"* he says. The source of this anguish is the awful scene showing on the black and white television. It is 1963 and President Kennedy has just been shot, gunned down on a sunny day in Texas, sending the world into crisis and mourning. The Cold War is at its height and everyone fears the Soviet Union and the atom bomb. In our childhood games, the 'reds' or the 'commies' are always the baddies. On the television, we have seen pictures of protests against the H-bomb and the fear of nuclear war pervades even children's lives.

∞

My father was too young to fight in the Second World War but entered National Service in 1946. Despite having a good time himself, playing in a band to the troops in India, he had lost friends and colleagues and the war was still very close. His father had fought in the First World War and there were only twenty years between the two wars, so it was perfectly imaginable that the world would, once again, become mired in conflict. His reasoning was perfectly logical. In 1961 the USSR had built 'the Berlin Wall' between East and West Berlin to stop the exodus of East Berliners to the West, the more prosperous sectors of the city run by the Americans, the British and the French. The West was reluctant to stop the building of the wall, fearing another war but their aim to destroy communism remained. The disastrous 'Bay of Pigs' invasion backed by the new president, John F. Kennedy, led directly to the Cuban Missile Crisis in 1962. It was not hard to believe that Kennedy's assassination was the work of the Soviet Union. In the event, of course, it proved to be a lone gunman, but the world teetered on the edge of terror for a while.

This was not the only time Dad talked to me about the world in which we lived. Despite my youth, he never talked down to me, but explained as best he could what was happening. He read the newspaper every day and followed the political life of the country passionately. I knew, even if I did not always understand, about Britain's role in the world and our responsibilities. I realised much later that his attitude was influenced by his upbringing, *the Daily Express* and the huge number of war films produced in the 1950s and 60s, where Britain was always portrayed as the plucky little nation battling alone to beat 'the Hun'. Winston Churchill, the great leader who 'won the war', was still alive and an even more personal hero for my father. He grew up with his father working at the Treasury (Office of HM Procurator General and Treasury Solicitor) under 'Winnie', holding the office of Higher Executive Officer for which he received an OBE in the 1951 New Year's Honours. They were a very traditional, conservative, middle-class family.

In 1953, Ian Fleming published his first 'James Bond' novel, *Casino Royale,* introducing a very British hero fighting a secret war against the communist enemy. James Bond was the perfect sophisticate who provided 'a fictional brand of great power nostalgia'. He fitted my father's ideal and that of many who continued to believe that to be British was somehow to be superior and having won the lottery of life. Britain still considered itself a world power and, in 1954, decided that it must have an independent nuclear deterrent as it could not continue to be a world power without one. The Suez crisis in 1956 brought a rude awakening. When Britain, along with France and Israel, invaded Egypt to recover control of the Suez Canal, its humiliating climbdown highlighted Britain's declining power and confirmed it as a 'second-tier' world power. But not for my father, who remained a patriotic defender of the status quo for the rest of his life.

By 1960, Britain's Empire was severely diminished but was still a source of labour for large public organisations. In 1956, London Transport became the first organisation to recruit staff directly from the Caribbean. They were followed by British Rail and the NHS. We loved the friendly 'coloured' as they were then known, bus drivers, train guards and nurses, there were many in Kingston on the outskirts of London. But while Mum embraced the growing diversity in our society, Dad was unsure. Though always polite he was uncomfortable, and thought they were taking the jobs of British workers which would only lead to trouble in the future. We may have seen many immigrants in our daily lives, but they were not part of our schools, our church or my parents' social lives.

Those social lives were dominated by music, weekend nights of playing jazz far and wide, often in Working Men's Clubs, but always white and predominantly male. Women were only grudgingly included and the frequent battles between my parents were as much to do with equality as anything else. The Dagenham Women's Strike, which eventually led to the Equal Pay Act, did not take place until 1968 and women were expected to stay at home with the children and provide a clean house, good food on the table and support for their breadwinner husbands. Any, preferably part-time, jobs they did were considered to be for pin money.

The more or less continuous 'war of words' between my parents had a lot to do with both politics and the rising expectations of working-class women. My maternal grandmother, Granny Stillwell, was strong, opinionated and staunchly Labour. Many of the women in our family have inherited that strong streak and we commonly say "she's a Stillwell" down the generations. Granny sang in the local Wesleyan choir and, though living a typical woman's life between the wars, she was vocal about women saying what they thought and girls being equal to boys. Her three daughters were far stronger characters and, arguably, more intelligent than her son. My mother was the youngest and possibly the one with most ambition. Sadly for her, she had passed the entrance exam to Chichester High School but there was no money to buy a school uniform in 1939 and bigger things for the family to worry about with another war on the horizon. Both her sisters joined the armed forces during the Second World War, and, according to my mother, had more exciting lives. They both subsequently married servicemen so it was a huge blow to her when, at the age of 17, her mother refused to allow her to marry a young Canadian soldier she had fallen in love with. It was probably for the best but Mum was determined to break away from her mother's control, something she did not understand with me, some 25 years later. Luckily for us, it led to her leaving home, moving to London and marrying my father. However, what she saw as her lack of achievement, was a constant itch and one she tried to assuage by encouraging my father to 'better himself'. She passed her strength, and probably some of her weaknesses, on to her daughters. She was very keen for her girls to achieve and was proud, but also a little jealous, when I passed the Eleven Plus exam in 1964. I could take up the grammar school education that had been denied her, though, to my regret, this did not extend beyond the age of 16 when she felt I had received 'enough education' and should go out and make a living, passing a large proportion of my salary to her for rent.

In 1963, the year before we moved house and I passed the Eleven Plus, Britain had been under Conservative rule for thirteen years. Despite the blip of a reforming socialist government from 1945-51, which introduced the welfare state, the nation had returned to the safe, traditional, conservative ideal of government. All that was about to change in the form of the clever Labour leader, Harold Wilson. Despite an Oxford education, Wilson played up his humble roots and Yorkshire background. The 1964-70 Labour government carried out a broad range of reforms in areas such as social security, civil liberties, housing, health, education and workers' rights. It was also a very liberal government, introducing the partial decriminalisation of male homosexuality and abortion, reform of the divorce laws and the abolition of theatre censorship and capital punishment. It introduced legislation addressing race relations and racial discrimination and made reforms to education, notably the expansion of comprehensive education and the creation of the Open University. All excellent initiatives one would think but these liberal reforms were the source of heated arguments in our house. My father was horrified by many of them and could see his safe, familiar world, falling apart. This was also, of course, the time of the 'Swinging 60s' and sexual liberation following the introduction of the contraception pill. As far as Dad was concerned, the country was "going to the dogs".

This attitude was brilliantly portrayed in the BBC1 series *Till Death Us Do Part* which began in the summer of 1966. It follows a working-class family, the Garnetts, who live in a terraced house in the shabby streets of East London. The head of the family is the irascible Alf, a staunch supporter of the monarchy and the Conservative Party who ceaselessly complains about left-wingers, do-gooders, 'darkies' and 'wogs'. This is completely unacceptable now, but these were common complaints in the 1960s and certainly chimed with many of my father's opinions. Dad loved the programme, it spoke for him and, interestingly, it allowed my parents to see that their differences were not unique. Alf Garnett's long-suffering wife and daughter constantly challenged his views and his left-wing son-in-law provided the political balance. The show captured a key feature of Britain in the 1960s: the public perception that the generation gap was widening. Alf's daughter and son-in-law supported aspects of the new era such as relaxed sexual mores, fashions and music, all things which were anathema to Alf and indicative of everything that was wrong with the younger generation and the liberal attitudes they embraced

Despite Dad's attitudes however, he rarely railed against his children, perhaps unfairly leaving the hard work of discipline to Mum. He did not agree with much of the new thinking but as I grew up, he tried to be a peacemaker between Mum and I and wanted a quieter life. There was certainly a generation gap in our house. My mother had been brought up with the maxim "children should be seen and not heard" and although this was very difficult in a house of four women, what Mum said had to be obeyed. If we questioned her actions, it was "do as I say, not as I do". My effrontery in saying this was hypocritical infuriated her and she always had the last word, being able to hold the threat of withdrawing privilege, whether it was a trip out with a friend, a night out at the youth club or even going to church. She was not a churchgoer herself and believed that "charity begins at home". My teenage years were a battlefield strewn with the ruins of our relationship.

Many battles resulted from me not being allowed to do something, often because I was required to babysit but not always. There didn't always have to be a reason and, sadly, reasonable discussion never seemed to take place. It was simply not acceptable to disagree and it was certainly not acceptable to complain outside the home. It was our business and no-one else's and I was in dreadful trouble if it was found out I had talked to 'outsiders' as I often did.

Was I so difficult? It is impossible to know, the only people who still remember my teenage life were on my side of course. I know I was independent and had a mind of my own, but I wish we had learnt to talk about our disagreements instead of bottling them up until an explosion took place. The trouble was, my opinion was irrelevant. Mum was totally in control of us all and it was: "my house, my rules".

∞

And while war raged in our house, so it did in the nation. In 1966, the Labour Government under the incumbent Prime Minister, Harold Wilson, won an increased majority in the House of Commons. The economy was slowly growing with a voluntary incomes policy agreed with the trade unions in place. George Brown, originally a trade unionist, but by now on the right of the party, was Deputy Leader and it was his Prices and Incomes policy that was now challenged by the National Union of Seamen. In order to uphold the policy and, by implication, the principles of sound economic management, Harold Wilson decided to stand determined against what he saw as the thin end of the wedge. After months of fruitless negotiations, Wilson raised the stakes with a speech in the Commons that stunned his supporters. Although never using the word 'Communists' everyone knew what he meant[1] This was the beginning of many years of strikes in the UK throughout the 1960s and 1970s.

One landmark dispute was the Ford sewing-machinists' women's strike at Dagenham in 1968. The women made car seat covers so their strike for equal pay meant that supplies for the cars eventually ran out. The strike was settled fairly quickly with a rise in pay for the women, though not to the level of the skilled men. This was due in the main to Barbara Castle, the Secretary of State for Employment and

---
[1] Family Britain

Productivity in Harold Wilson's government and this strike ultimately led to the Equal Pay Act 1970. There were fireworks in our house! It was normal practice for women to be paid less than men, even for doing the same job and my father was of the old school belief that a woman's place was in the home and if she did work, it was only for 'pin money'. This was somewhat hypocritical as Mum had worked since we were all at school and, though this was only ever part-time, was mainly responsible for the savings which enabled them to buy their own house and for us to have regular holidays. Mum was, unsurprisingly, thrilled by the inspiring Barbara Castle and by the success of the women strikers. The arguments were superfluous really. Dad was quite happy with equality in practice, but not in theory. He had three daughters and he wanted us all to succeed, just as long as he didn't have to change.

In 1972, the miners went out on strike for the first time since 1926. The country depended on coal and, for a time, they were the highest paid amongst the working classes. However, their actions resulted in Margaret Thatcher's war on the unions and the gradual decline of Britain's industrial base. For us though, it was more personal. Dad worked for Charrington's Coal Merchants, collecting regular weekly amounts from housewives for their coal and part of his pay was commission. Money worries resulted and, for once, my parents agreed on politics.

Despite the fact that Dad's jazz band evenings brought in much needed extra money, it was still a source of much strife between my parents. By the mid-1960s Dad had changed to playing the drums and the huge space on the top of the wardrobe in my sisters' room was taken up with his drum set.

He still played every Friday and Saturday nights and it became even more of bone of contention between them. As I grew older and attended clubs in the evening, Mum resented it even more. It had a knock-on effect on me as she began to expect me to babysit on occasion, instead of attending Girls' Brigade or the church youth club. I resented this bitterly and there were many tears from me and arguments which only added fuel to the fire of my resentment.

∞

Looking back, the second decade of my life, and our move to Tolworth, was a process of separation and detachment, though natural, but not always welcome, from the family. I see myself, as if looking through a lens, as slightly separate and often alone. They were a family of four with me as an awkward, and often bad-tempered addition and there were many trips out without me. This was perhaps inevitable, given the family make-up and the deteriorating relationship between Mum and me, but it contributed a great deal to the unhappiness that seemed to pervade my teenage years. I realise now that I was jealous of my sisters almost from the day they were born. Twins are so appealing and instead of being the loved only child, I was now the odd one out. They were pretty too, with long, blonde hair while mine was mousy and it didn't help when Mum told me that I had the brains, while they had the beauty. I felt they had both! Having to stay home to babysit meant that I resented them which wasn't fair at all, it wasn't their fault.

It seems inevitable now: my distress at leaving my childhood home; my return to the town of my birth every day to go to the grammar school; my friends from far and wide; my widening horizons; all increasing the gap; as against a family happy in their new life in their own house with two lovely little girls who were far more biddable than I would ever be. As Mum said I was "getting above myself".

Notes:

1 Family Britain p267
2 https://www.ourmigrationstory.org.uk/oms/london-on-the-move-west-indian-transport-workers
3 & 4 White Heat, Dominic Sandbrook
5 https://en.wikipedia.org/wiki/Till_Death_Us_Do_Part
6 Family Britain

Chapter Three
A Saxon Town

The cobbled streets and gabled roofs of Kingston now are gone
   And Saxon glories are but ghosts raised faintly by a stone
   But ever Father Thames flows on past bridge and wharf and quay
   And overall the Red Stone Tower stands plain for all to see.

So goes the second verse of the Tiffin Girls' School song which we sing every school birthday. There are still some cobbled streets and gabled roofs in the market place, along with the Coronation Stone and, from here, you can see the red stone tower of the Guildhall. My schoolfriend Sheila and I are in Woolworth's deciding whether to buy a pair of stockings or a 'single', also known as a '45' pop record. They both cost 1/11d and we can only afford one or the other.

∞

Many years later at a reunion, an old friend said she remembered I lived in Tolworth. "Oh, but I have always been a Kingston girl," I re-joined.

The town of my birth has always been special to me. Having spent the first ten years of my life there and not wanting to leave, the fact that I was back a year later at the Grammar School meant I felt I never really left. It was both ancient and modern, traditional yet forward-looking and it seemed to reflect the person I was already aware of becoming in 1964 when I arrived in the first year of Tiffin Girls' School.

In Saxon times, Kingston was known as 'Cyninges tun' Old English meaning King's manor or King's farm and by 1086 was mentioned in the Doomsday Book as Chingestune. Over the years this gradually changed to become *Kingeston,* then *Kingestowne upon Thames*. This ancient town, the earliest Royal Borough, was located on the borders of the ancient kingdoms of Wessex and Mercia which made it the ideal coronation spot. The beautiful All Saints' Church, where I was christened and now, thanks to my sister Ali, have a memorial tile on the floor, was on the site of an important estate of the West Saxon Kings and host to Royal coronations. The Coronation Stone itself is linked to the coronation of eight Saxon kings (although strangely, the Stone has nothing to do with the town's name). In 1793 a London guidebook reported that it was the stone on which the Saxon kings sat while being crowned. The most well-known of these kings was Athelstan, the first ruler who could truly be considered King of England. After being crowned in Kingston in 925 AD, Athelstan defeated the Scots and Vikings, unifying regional kingdoms into one nation. Kingston was the place where England began.

The ancient market place was a thriving, bustling place. With its Tudor, gabled buildings, its myriad market stalls selling everything from fruit and vegetables, fish and meat to a wide range of materials for just about every home project, and every high street shop imaginable, it was, and still is, the heart of the town. Getting the 65 bus from school into town, we would often stop off to wander round the shops before getting the 406 home. It was the beginning of the age of the teenager and, although we did not have a lot of money to spend, there was plenty to tempt us. Once at school in Kingston, I had more freedom as long as I was home in time for tea.

Kingston market place c.1960
Francis Frith photos

Another after school favourite occupation was a visit to the Coronation Swimming Baths. By the time it closed in 1979 it had become very old-fashioned, but back in the 1960s it was a wonderful facility with three pools and one of the highest diving boards in the country. It was always busy, there wasn't a great deal else to do for teenagers and it was a real treat to go swimming with friends, finishing off with a hot Bovril in the modern café afterwards. As our mothers repeatedly told us, we were so lucky, they never had such things to do in their day, nor the time to meet friends. We were living a different life and our mothers were quite jealous.

Kingston's ancient coat of arms shows three salmon representing the three fisheries of Kingston mentioned in the Domesday Book. The three fishes can still be found throughout the town and were on our school badge. More interesting to us as teenagers was The Three Fishes pub, the unofficial marijuana dispensary of Kingston during the 1960s and 70s (later renamed the Royal Charter but eventually demolished in the 1980s to build a relief road). It was on the corner of Richmond Road, opposite the Odeon cinema and was also known for its hippies, loud music and fights between Mods and Rockers. I was warned never to go there and was far too frightened of my mother to disobey, even if I had wanted to. In fact, despite everyone knowing it was a drugs haunt, I somehow never seemed to know anyone who had actually been there or indeed taken any drugs. Of course, a Tiffin Girl would never do such a thing! We had it drummed into us that we were representing the school when we were out in public and woe betide any girl who took off her beret or misbehaved in any way. There would always be a teacher or prefect on the bus you hadn't seen who would report you. Once I graduated to college in 1969, however, it was a different story.

Kingston has changed much over the years. Although there were many familiar landmarks in my youth and much of the town remained as it had been for centuries, there was a great deal of new building in the 1950s when many old landmarks were pulled down to make way for the new. The decade saw a gradual beginning of the end for industries that had dominated the local economy, in particular along the riverside which was slowly becoming a fine promenade with leisure facilities and parkland, our beloved Canbury Gardens.

The path to the Gardens across from our house was a wide, tree lined avenue in those days, separating the power station from the Gardens. But in 1994 the power station was demolished and planning permission given for housing on the site. On 25 March 1998 the beautiful poplars separating the park from the Fairclough Homes site were felled, a cause which had resulted in protests, an eco-warrior camp, and a 17,000-person petition. The Surrey Comet reported that: "The first of the Canbury Gardens' poplars came crashing down on Wednesday evening after a massive eviction operation costing up to £500,000 and involving 300 police, bailiffs, privacy security men, helicopters and boats."

Path from Kings Road to Canbury Gardens

The magic pathway I remember was gone. Its dappled path and ancient trees were like going 'through the wardrobe'[2] for me. Mum would wheel the pram down on summer afternoons and we would have a round on the putting green, followed by a strawberry Mivvi, but I was also allowed to go there on my own and would escape to wander along the riverside or curl up on the grass to read. Too far to go alone, but another favourite place, was Bushy Park, close to Hampton Court Palace. A bus ride away, it was a real treat in the school holidays, offering a large paddling pool, sandpit and lots of space to run around. Just like in Richmond Park, the huge antlers of deer hiding in amongst the ancient oaks were a common sight.

∞

There have been bridges across the Thames since the 12th century and there have been markets in Kingston since the early 1200s. The ancient market place in the centre of town provided our fruit and vegetables and fresh fish on Fridays, but mum preferred to shop when I was at school. Two babies were quite enough and, although it was a good twenty minute walk into town, it would be impossible to board a trolley bus with the heavy Silver Cross twin pram. There were no folding buggies then. The trolley buses with their overhead electric lines had replaced trams soon after the war and they, in their turn, were replaced by the Route master buses from 1962. When I was born in 1953, the Cattle Market in the Fairfield area was still trading livestock but by 1957 this had ceased and become a regular Monday market.

Also, in Fairfield was one of my favourite places of all, the library. Kingston was the second place in Greater London to adopt the Libraries Act and Kingston Library opened in temporary accommodation in 1882. The site in Fairfield Road was acquired in 1899 and money was raised to build a new public library. The cost of the building exceeded the estimate and a further £2000, a huge sum in those days, was donated by Andrew Carnegie, a Scottish-American industrialist and philanthropist, then the richest man in the world and funder of over two and a half thousand public libraries around the world. I knew nothing about that then of course. I just knew I felt more comfortable there than anywhere else as a child. From the age of 6 or 7, Mum would drop me off at the library while she shopped with the twins and I would sit on the wooden floor and lose myself in the worlds that books opened up. She was a great reader herself, though she had little time for reading then and, although I don't remember her reading to me, she could not have given me a better introduction to books than to leave me regularly in the library. She, like me, felt that libraries were special, safe places and no one seemed to think it odd then that such a young child would be left there, sometimes for a couple of hours.

Children had much less supervision in the 1950s and 60s and there was a lot less traffic so I was not unusual in walking alone, or sometimes catching the bus, to school, church or into town, even before the age of 10. Soon after I started school in 1958, I also started going to Sunday School at the Methodist Church on the Richmond Road. It was opposite my school where I walked every day but it meant crossing the busy main road. Dad would walk up to the top of our road and cross me over so that I walked safely along the other side until I reached the church. There I met friends who, though we lost touch during the years after I moved to Tolworth, became part of my social group many years later when I attended the youth club at Surbiton Hill Methodist church.

Kingston Methodist Sunday School class c. 1960

Children had chores to do if we wanted our pocket money. Helping out with the twins was the most common of mine but it was a real treat to be asked to return empty bottles to the grocer's shop. The Milkman sold lemonade and orange juice but, just occasionally, Dad would buy a bottle of ginger beer or Tizer and I would take the empty bottles back and be allowed to keep the penny deposit on each. Even back then though, the smaller shops were disappearing with the building of more and bigger stores in the town. Over the Christmas 1953 season, Kingston drew an unprecedented number of shoppers. A poll by the *Surrey Comet* found four main reasons: variety of shops (more than Croydon, Sutton or Guildford), exciting window displays, bargains in the Market Place and good public transport. This was despite a threatened rail strike which prompted panic posting of Christmas cards and parcels. Kingston Central Post Office took on 600 temporary workers who, with the regular staff, handled a record amount of mail the week before Christmas.

The most important shop of all, to me at least, was Bentalls, its graceful curved building dominating the heart of Kingston.

Bentalls of Kingston
(Photo taken in 2011)

It was one of the largest and best department stores in the south of England and, no doubt, contributed a huge amount to Kingston's popularity as a shopping centre. Its Blue Cross winter and summer sales were legendary and people would queue all night for the best bargains. Unlike today, when 'sales' seem to be permanent, prices really were hugely reduced and there were bargains to be had. In the 1950s, when I went there as a child, mothers could leave their babies in beautiful coach built prams at the side entrance. A nurse in a stiff, starched uniform was on duty to look after the babies while their mothers shopped at leisure. My earliest memory of Bentalls was of having my hair cut on the brightly coloured carousel horses, but it became special too over the years for the visits to buy a Sunday dress and later to be kitted out proudly in my uniform for the grammar school. Even after we moved to Tolworth, we would get the 406 bus to Kingston to shop at Bentalls and tea in the Silver Café was a real treat. It had celebrity attraction too. Singer Petula Clark gave her first public performance in Bentalls, singing as a child with an orchestra in Bentall's entrance hall and there was still music in the foyer on a regular basis adding to the stylish upmarket feel of the store. In the 1950s and 60s it was popular with women of the growing middle classes and its genteel, yet stylish modernity meant it was not unusual to see well known models trying out the new fashions, in particular those of Mary Quant whose designs were all the rage. The Bentall Centre today keeps the name alive and, indeed, the store is still there but it has none of the magic and grandeur of that earlier store. Kingston's shops continued to attract record numbers. With the opening of one of the new Habitat stores in 1967 the town enhanced its reputation for style and modernity.

∞

I am tired but happy. I have just finished my first day as a shop assistant at Littlewoods in Kingston. I felt very grown up, travelling in on the bus, not to school, but to my first proper job. I worked at the Tolworth bakery for a while but this is different. I have a smart uniform, I have to clock in and out like all the other women and I am treated like an adult. There is a staff canteen where we have our lunch and there is time to go shopping in our break too. It is exhausting being on my feet behind the mens' trousers counter for eight hours a day, but I am paid the princely sum of 15 shillings for the day.

I can begin to buy my own clothes, instead of Mum choosing them for me which, at the age of 15 is very embarrassing.

Notes:

1 Canbury Gardens Design Report February 2020
2 Kingston in the 50's by June Sampson and Mark Davison
3 White Heat by Dominic Sandbrook
4 15 shillings is 75p in 2020

Chapter Four
High Days and Holidays

It is the start of the summer holidays and I am beside myself with excitement. I am waiting at the bus stop at the top of the road with Mum and soon I will be getting on the Southdown coach to take me all the way to Southsea to stay with my cousins. The butterflies in my tummy are a sign of my nervousness and the excitement of the adventure. I will spend the three hour journey sitting behind the driver who will look after me when we stop at Hindhead for a tea break and then deliver me safely to my aunt and cousin Lindy at the bus stop in Southsea. In a week's time, Lindy and I will travel back to Kingston where we will spend another week together at my house. We do this every summer and it is the highlight of my year. Tomorrow Lindy and I will take our towels and a picnic down to the pebbly beach and love our freedom, away from her little brother and my little sisters, and, most of all, from our strict mothers who we love but want to get away from too. We spend hours on the beach before wandering back through the quiet streets to their house in Prince Albert Road, hot and tired, but happy. If we have a few pennies to spare, we will buy a blue ice jubbly from the corner shop.

∞

It seems incredible to me now that a child of 9 or 10 would be put on a bus for a three hour journey, without any adult supervision apart from the bus driver, but so it was, and probably not uncommon in the early 1960s. We were so lucky to have cousins who lived by the sea and they, in turn, thought it was wonderful to have cousins who lived near London. It was a very satisfactory arrangement for everyone. Our mothers were sisters and very close, and those holidays laid the foundations for a lifelong sibling relationship between me and my cousin Lin, for which I am eternally grateful.

Lindy and Susie circa 1959

We were the closest in age but there was an extended family of cousins on the south coast which made our summers and Christmases wonderful occasions. Mum was a different person then, back in the bosom of her family and Dad too enjoyed the large and jolly family he never had. Until our Auntie Rose's death in 1961 our cousins Richard and Andy were sometimes part of these events, but after that, sadly, we did not see so much of them. I well remember though one visit by Richard to stay with us in Kingston. I was 12 and he was 18, just off to university which seemed a huge achievement for anyone in our class. I did not realise it then but of course his father was as middle class as mine but better educated, and, no doubt, understood the value of a good education. I was awestruck by this handsome, clever cousin, little knowing that would be the last time I saw him for 50 years! We were all brought together when a small inheritance from our bachelor uncle came to light in 2015.

My Auntie Joan and Uncle Aubrey had three children, seven years apart. My cousin Lindy was just a year older than me and her older sister Valerie, in her mid to late teens then, was someone I was secretly rather in awe of. She had a very impressive beehive hairdo, played pop music by her idol Anthony Newley, posters of whom were plastered all over her bedroom walls, and even went out with boys! She was very kind to her little cousin and I was so excited to be invited to be a bridesmaid at her wedding in 1964. The beautiful apricot dress was never worn by me, sadly. I contracted chicken pox and had to watch from a distance while another little girl took my place. Lindy's little brother Michael was about the same age as my sisters but as he was no threat to me, I found him rather sweet. I'd always wanted a brother in any case though I am sure he didn't take kindly to me and Lindy insisting he play the baby in our games.

Those summers in the house in Prince Albert Road were magical. Having a holiday of my own away from home, spending hours on the beach and, best of all, a playmate my own age, it was not surprising that I longed for the summer holidays. It was not so easy to be independent when Lindy came to stay with me. While we lived in Kingston, we went to Canbury Gardens on our own but when we moved to Tolworth in 1964, there were fewer places to go to a safe walk away. Although it was a lot quieter in the 1960s than it is in the 21st century, we were still on the outskirts of London rather than in a quiet seaside town. However, it was a good opportunity to go out and Mum would take us to Hampton Court or Bushy Park and, of course, a favourite occupation, shopping in Bentalls.

Christmas too was special. The families would take turns to spend it in Southsea or in Kingston. Christmas Eve was a half day holiday so we would pack up the old Ford Pop(ular) and head down to the coast. The houses were not big, but we all squeezed in somehow, the children sleeping top to toe in beds and sharing the bedroom with numerous cousins. The stairs in Prince Albert Road were steep and there was no question of going down for the toilet before the upstairs bathroom was built so, of course, there was the obligatory potty or gazunder under the bed. It was in those years that the giving of Christmas tree presents began for the children. We would have been up and opened our presents very early on Christmas morning so by tea time on Boxing Day we were bored and troublesome. The promise of a tree present after tea kept us in line, a tradition that lasted in our family until only a few years ago when we realised we were trying to cram three or four days of traditions into one day!

I have always loved Christmas and I am sure it is, in no small part, due to the fact that my mother did too. She shed her often cross exterior and became almost childlike in her excitement and enjoyment of the season. Though not a keen cook, her speciality was pastry and she would roll up her sleeves and make tray after tray of scrumptious mince pies, the pastry melting in your mouth and the fruit overflowing and burning your lips if you ate them while they were hot. There was not a lot of money to spare but we always had a sack overflowing with presents at the foot of our bed, albeit most of them had been sent by our generous aunts and uncles and grandparents. There would always be an orange and some golden chocolate coins in our stocking and the latest favourite annual: Beano followed by Judy or Bunty as I grew older. I did not have any dolls that I remember, preferring more practical and tomboyish pursuits, no doubt due to Dad's treating me like the son he did not have. One year we spent all day building houses with a Meccano-like house building set, the next taking pictures with my Kodak Brownie camera. I am sure Mum would have appreciated some help with the Christmas dinner, especially as Dad would have gone out to the pub beforehand, but on those occasions she bit her tongue and let him play, no doubt keeping us all out from under her feet.

The Christmas lights in London's Oxford and Regent Streets were a magical sight to a child, especially one growing up in the grey post war years, and, once Dad had a car, we were taken into London to see them every year. Winter Sundays were also a time to drive into London and visit the free museums: the Science Museum and the Natural History Museum with its distinctive skeleton of a blue whale were favourites. There were no shops open on Sundays of course, so the streets were quiet and almost empty of traffic.

Even though we lived close to my paternal grandparents, we saw very little of them. Sadly my Grandad died when I was only three and although I sometimes think I can picture his jolly face, I suspect it is rather from photos of him. He and my Nana were solidly middle-class. Grandad, William Ewart Pegg (Ewart after Gladstone, the Victorian Prime Minister), had excelled himself in the army during World War I, mentioned in dispatches "for gallant and distinguished services in the field". There followed an illustrious career in the Civil Service, which culminated in him being awarded an MBE in the 1951 New Year's Honours, acknowledged by a letter of congratulation from the then Chancellor of the Exchequer, Hugh Gaitskell. He courted Edith Elizabeth Cox, my Nana, during the war when she was an Observer for the Royal Flying Corps and sent her a beautiful embroidered postcard from the front for her 21st birthday in 1916.

They did not marry until 1922 though their life was one of middle-class society, privilege and gaiety. Nana loved parties and fun but when she gave birth to a son, marked by a strawberry birthmark in 1926, she transferred all her passion and energy into protecting him from life. Terrified of a repeat of the birthmark in another child, he remained their only, much loved and spoilt, child. Her darling husband, Billie, pandered to her in this and many other ways, protecting them both from the realities of life. The shock was immense therefore when, at the age of only 64, he died from a heart attack, for my Nana to discover that their house was rented, not owned. Luckily for her, his generous civil service pension ensured she was reasonably comfortable. Financially secure but sadly, not emotionally. Having poured her life into her son, she found it difficult to share him with a wife. She and my mother did not get on and visits to see her were rare. I liked her but probably because she tried to spoil me too, making beautiful party dresses and sending lavish presents, much to my mother's annoyance.

My mother's parents were very different indeed and seemed much older. This was probably partly because Granny Stillwell walked with a pronounced limp, the result of a broken leg as a child which had never been set properly. Despite that, and her short stature, she was a scary figure, dominating everyone, child or adult, in the family. But underneath that harsh exterior, there were flashes of kindness and a summer visit to stay with her and Grandad and their bachelor son, Uncle Arthur, brings back good memories: shelling peas, going shopping and helping to prepare the dinner, making pastry and singing hymns. Granny sang for the local Wesleyan choir and had a lovely voice. Her Methodist background was somewhat at odds with her passion for horse racing and betting on the horses was the cause of many an argument with my Grandad. Robert Henry, my Grandad, was a very kind man, with a twinkle in his eyes and laughter brimming over. His passion was his garden and he proudly grew prize vegetables and dahlias. He had an older sister named Susie and I felt very special in sharing this family name. He and Granny had married during the war in 1916 and my mother was the youngest of their four children. By the time I came along, they had many grandchildren and we were the London family that lived furthest away, so our visits to them were also rare, despite the regular visits to the aunt, uncle and cousins just down the road in Portsmouth. There was much more of a generation gap in those days and also a sense that, once you were married, you had to stand on your own two feet and get on with life, even though most people married young in their teens or early 20s.

Our visits to Portsmouth were only possible once we had a car, something of a luxury in the 1960s, and a result of our father's job as a representative. Many families did not own one, the roads were quiet and there were no motorways so journeys took many hours. Despite the distances, we travelled annually down to the West Country for holidays, leaving Kingston in the middle of the night, my sisters and I wrapped in blankets and squashed into the back of the car, while Dad drove for up to ten hours if we were going down to our favourite destination, Newquay in Cornwall which was the genteel holiday destination of 1960s Britain. The car smelt of exhaust fumes and there were no seatbelts, though we were so squashed together we couldn't move in any case, but it was a terrific adventure and, once awake, and having stopped for tea and sandwiches for breakfast, we would sing our way to our destination at the tops of our voices. Mum loved to sing too and we knew songs from all the shows and latest films, our favourites being from the Sound of Music and Mary Poppins. We knew the journey up and down the A3, A30 and A303 by our own landmarks: the Long Tunnel at Esher, Stonehenge, the dreadful queues through the town of Honiton before its by-pass, then across the Tamar into Cornwall and, the 'nearly there' landmark of Jamaica Inn, made famous by Daphne du Maurier in the book of the same name published in 1936. It has become something of a rather tacky tourist destination now but then it was a ramshackle old pub which you could well imagine harboured smugglers.

Our holidays in Devon and Cornwall were magical times, not least because we had Dad all day every day. For the rest of the year, we saw little of him, his day job and musical life taking much of his time. It is not difficult to understand now why our mother was frequently ill-tempered but then I longed for the odd days out and the holidays which made the family dynamics more even, and of course for Dad's attention. One particular favourite location was the family run farmhouse at Combe Martin where we holidayed more than once. The huge breakfasts and wonderful creamy milk from the farm meant Dad was happy whereas staying in the country for Mum was a return to her youth. Devon has that wonderful mix of country and coast which is what she had grown up with in Chichester and still loved. After a day on the beach and a hearty tea, we would go for a walk along the country lanes in the evening sunshine and Mum would breathe in the smell of manure happily while the rest of us held our noses!

We didn't realise it then, but we were luckier than many children of our generation in having not just one, but often two holidays a year. Mum was a great saver and worked as soon as my sisters went to school. To her we owed our treats and holidays though I doubt I was ever grateful. Rather than spend the money on staying in our Combe Martin farmhouse once each year, we began to have two holidays, but in a caravan, or in fact static mobile homes, set in parks with lots to do and a bar for the evening. Going away at Easter became a great treat, the cooler and shorter days meant that we were allowed to go to the café/bar after tea and have a packet of crisps and a coca cola in its distinctive glass bottle – the height of sophistication.

There were days out from home too. Our parents' friends, Pete and Doreen and their daughter Linda had a much better car than us and often joined us on trips to West Wittering beach in Sussex. Linda was only a couple of years older than me so I was sometimes invited to travel in their car, rather than squashed into the smelly old Ford Pop with my sisters – it was heaven. Whether it was a day out at Wittering or a week or two in Devon or Cornwall, we spent a great many hours on the beach. Dad was a wizard at building huge sandcastles, fantastic structures with long, winding runs for a tennis ball which we delighted in playing with right up until the tide took the castle away: we begged to remain until the tide came in, often staying on the beach into the evening when the sea was warm and the crowds were gone, before heading back, tired and often sunburnt, for tea. I was lucky in that I turned a berry brown quite easily but Dad frequently used to have burnt feet from kneeling down building sandcastles, not many people used sun cream then.

Mum and Dad were sociable people and had many friends. Along with Pete and Doreen, they had a great card cartel with Johnny & Marge and spent Sunday evenings with them for many years, either at the pub or at our house playing cards. Johnny was a bit of a charmer and flirted with my mother shamelessly. He and Marge had no children of their own and he often used to bring us small presents like a favourite uncle. There were parties too, and it was a real treat to be taken to stay at Pete and Doreen's house in Ewell for a New Year's Eve party. We had our own 'midnight feast' upstairs and were thoroughly spoilt. Their house was like a mansion to us, with its own bar room where the grown-ups mixed cocktails and the women danced while the men played jazz into the small hours. The cigarette smoke wafted up the stairs as we watched through the banisters until we almost fell asleep on the floor.

Mum's best friend was Sheila, my godmother, who had three children of her own, Mark, Jayne and Lawrence, though Lawrence was born after I stopped joining them on the regular visits for tea. Once I went to secondary school, it was too far for me to get there after school. However, another friend, Margaret and her husband Fred, lived in Surbiton which was on my way home and so I made my way to Villiers Avenue on a regular visit, something I came to hate. They were a very different family to us and quite intellectual. Their house was full of books and it was taken for granted that their son Paul would go to university. He was quite arrogant about it and I rather resented the implication that I wouldn't, not because I wasn't clever enough but because Mum said there was no chance of affording it, even though in those days there were no student loans, fees were paid in full by local education authorities and there was a means-tested annual grant to cover living costs. I clearly remember overhearing her and Margaret arguing about whether I should be given the chance but Mum was determined I shouldn't 'get above myself'.

When I went to secondary school in 1964, my sisters were only 6, by the time I left in 1969 just 11. It is not surprising then, that I spent very little time with them during my teenage years and grew further and further apart from my family. As often as I could, I spent time with friends after school, often staying for tea and then coming home to spend the evening doing my homework. Holidays became less of a pleasure, I was often accused of being 'bolshy' which I probably was, preferring my own company and a book to joining in with family fun. By the time I was 16, they were going away without me while I had my best friend, Sheila, to stay with me. We got up to some high jinks – but that's another story!

∞

I am sitting on the stairs in our dark hallway; the black Bakelite telephone sits on the table and next to it, a dark blue passport. I can't quite believe that they are having the first family holiday abroad without me. I didn't really want to go, and I don't blame them for not wanting me to go with them, but still I feel hurt. This really does seem like the end of an era. I shall get my own passport and go away with my friends to celebrate my 18th birthday in a few months' time. Meanwhile, I have a fortnight of freedom and the house to myself which is reason for celebration now. I refuse to be upset, I have my own life to lead.

Notes:

1 Guardian Education: https://www.theguardian.com/politics/2003/jan/23/uk.education

2 In the late 1960s a family could all travel on one passport. This was common practice until the 1980s – The History of Multi-Passenger Passports – https://www.passport-collector.com/wp-content/uploads/AR17_Topol_21-24-.pdf

Chapter Five
Wonderland and Other Magical Worlds – Escapes into Reading

Christmas morning – a bulging sack is at the foot of the bed. Father Christmas has been but it is still very dark and we are not supposed to get up yet. I can see the shape of the present I want most of all so I very quietly wriggle down the bed, put my arm in and pull out my book. I know it's not really from Father Christmas because my Uncle Arthur buys me an Annual every year and I long for it. They are the only books I own and I read them over and over again. Even though we go to the library every week, I always run out of books to read.

∞

I don't remember learning to read. It seemed like I had always been able to and I devoured books of any type from a young age. Books with pictures were best and one of my early favourites was *Teddy Robinson* by Joan G. Robinson. Strangely, I did not have a teddy bear but that didn't matter because Teddy Robinson was as real to me as a real bear. Although I didn't own many books, we went to the library every week where there was an almost overwhelming choice. I was never ready to leave and agonized over which books to take home. Mum was a great reader, though I don't know how she found the time with three small children but she loved settling down with one of her favourite authors on a Saturday afternoon when we were old enough to amuse ourselves. There were not many books in our house but then libraries were used by most people and books were expensive. Dad had a few James Bond novels on the shelf by the fireplace but that was all. By the time I was 7 or 8 I had discovered comics and the Beano began to arrive every week to much joy and excitement. I particularly remember the first edition of 1961 because it was an 'upside down year' – you could turn the comic upside down and the year still read 1961! That led to the Christmas treat of the Annuals in my Christmas sack, first the Beano, then later Judy or Bunty, girls' comics first published in the late 1950s.

I began to receive books as birthday presents too. My lovely Auntie Rose sent me *Princess Margaret's Wedding Book* for my 7th birthday and the glorious colour photographs entranced me. For my 8th birthday I received something equally special: a 1957 Encyclopaedia, I did not even know such books existed. I pored over its pages and began to learn about the world I lived in. I travelled far and wide and learnt to dream. I read about things I did not understand and it awakened in me a hunger to learn.

As I progressed to books without pictures, I loved to read adventures. My first love was the *Milly-Molly-Mandy* stories by Joyce Lankester Brisley. Written in the 1920s they were quite dated: no cars or telephones, but that made them more exciting somehow. They told of a different world with different rules. Milly-Molly-Mandy roamed the countryside, having wonderful adventures, despite being very young (the books took her from the age of 4 to the age of 8), often without her parents. The best stories are the ones without adults and children's authors understand this. Children can get up to all sorts of mischief if there are no grownups around to spoil the fun. The difference then was that we really could get up to far more mischief than today's children. We had so much more freedom and would be out to play every day. No one worried as long as we were home by tea-time.

The best adventures though, were undoubtedly those of Enid Blyton. Despite the fact that she was banned from the BBC for nearly 30 years and, for many of those, from public libraries, for her "racism, bigotry and second-rate writing", she was incredibly popular with children. The formulaic and familiar stories were just what children loved, and still do. Which of the Famous Five you wanted to be depended on what type of person you were: I identified with Anne but really wanted to be George, the tomboy girl who was the most daring of them all. Blyton's stories painted girls and boys in stereotypical roles but then that reflected our lives. I read everything I could lay my hands on and though I enjoyed the school stories of *Malory Towers*, it was the Adventure and Mystery books I loved the most.

Enid Blyton also wrote many books for younger children and though I had seen them in the library, they did not appeal to me. *Noddy* was rather childish I thought and her *Golliwog* books were positively horrid. The original golliwog stories, written by Florence Upton in the early 20th century, had led to golliwog dolls being extremely popular throughout the century but Enid Blyton's golliwogs were nasty, mischievous creatures, often drawn as the villains of her stories. It would be unthinkable today to portray such creatures, no wonder she was deemed racist.

The Saturdays by Elizabeth Enright was another favourite read over and over again on wet Saturday afternoons. It was closer to my own life but I was rather envious of the four Melendy children with their ready-made playmates. Set in pre-war New York, it seemed more glamorous than dull and dreary early 1960s suburbia but I liked to imagine my Saturdays could be like theirs.

The best place to choose books from in the library was the 'returned books' trolley. There you could come across books and authors you had never heard of, knowing someone else had just read it. It was there, one memorable Saturday, that I found Edward Eager's *Half Magic*. Four children find a magical charm that has the power to grant wishes – but only half of every wish. This was a new genre for me and I loved it, best of all was Eager's *The Time Garden*. Four children (always four – I loved this and wanted to be in a family of four siblings, I even intended to have four of my own but stuck to two!) staying in the country one summer discover that the herb thyme can transport them back in time. Travelling throughout history from the American Civil War to Victorian England was dependent on which type of thyme they picked. I was hooked and my interest in history was awoken, never to dim. It led to a lifetime of reading historical fiction from which I learnt more history than I was ever taught in school.

And, of course, there was *Alice*. I don't remember when I first read *Alice in Wonderland* and *Through the Looking Glass* but I do know it was a revelation. *"We're all mad here,"* says the Cheshire Cat and for the first time I felt my sometimes-crazy imagination was something permissible, it was alright to be a little bit 'mad'. *Alice* is full of wonderful quotes and they have come unbidden to me many times in my life. *"Who are you?"* says the caterpillar. *"... I know who I was this morning, but I've changed several times since then."* I often felt I was a different person, depending on where I was and who I was with. As I've grown older, I have realized we all do that, but then it was a novel, and rather reassuring idea. *Alice* has been my go-to book ever since, its characters, humour and madness somehow making sense of many dilemmas. Over the years I have collected many editions and become interested in the various illustrators' depiction of these much-loved characters, but John Tenniel's originals are still unbeaten, in my mind at least. On my wall hangs a limited-edition print from John Tenniel's original lithograph, of Alice and the Cheshire Cat – it is one of my most prized possessions.

It seems that I wanted to live a different life and, in a way, I did. Every reader experiences numerous lives and places and reading was certainly an escape for me, but also a window onto different worlds, places and lives. When I read *Seven White Gates* by Malcolm Saville, I wanted to live in the wilds of Shropshire with its eerie Stiperstones mountains or, at least somewhere out in the country where you could hear the wind in the trees and imagine it was ghosts. There were trees along the streets where we lived and I was fond of them, but pollarded plane trees do not lend themselves to wind rushing through them.

There were books too which made me want to dance and sing. *Ballet Shoes* by Noel Streatfeild entranced me and I wanted to be Pauline, Petrova or Posy Fossil. I loved dancing,

Mum and I adored The Tiller Girls on Sunday Night at the London Palladium. This TV variety show, hosted by Bruce Forsyth from 1958-1964, was watched by millions of people and introduced big stars to our screens. Here we saw the Beatles before they were really famous, their appearance on the show heralding the beginning of 'Beatlemania'. The glamour of the stage was irresistible. In *The Swish of the Curtain* by Pamela Brown, seven children form the Blue Door Theatre Company, renovating a disused chapel and putting on plays in the summer holidays. If only my holidays were as exciting, but it did encourage me to get involved at school and church in some wonderful drama productions.

Starting at the Grammar school in 1964 opened my eyes to new worlds of literature. Homer's *The Odyssey* and *The Iliad* were my first introduction to the Greek myths and I soon discovered that there were many wonderful authors who wrote about ancient history. I began to read Geoffrey Trease, Rosemary Sutcliffe and numerous others, writing about events far in the past but bringing them to life on the page. From the ancient world to World War Two and everything in between, I gobbled it up. It wasn't always great literature but as long as it was a good story, it didn't matter. I learnt about all the royal houses of Europe reading Jean Plaidy and can still picture the complete royal family tree in my mind.

School introduced me to American & Canadian literature: I was *Anne of Green Gables*, sent by mistake to farmers who wanted to adopt a boy; *Tom Sawyer* and *Huckleberry Finn* in the racism of the pre-Civil war American south and Jo, (of course) in *Little Women.* I became *White Fang*, the wild wolfdog as he becomes domesticated. It mattered not whether the protagonist was female, male or animal. I became them all. The glamour of American literature was new to me as was the attraction of the television shows coming from 'across the pond': *The Waltons* was one such featuring the perfect family in the huge white porched houses still familiar across America today. Of course, in the library the books were arranged alphabetically which was often how I discovered new authors. One Saturday afternoon, having just finished *The Once and Future King* by T.H. White, a wonderful story of King Arthur, I sat down on the library floor at the W's to see if he had written any more. There I discovered my 'coming-of-age' novel: *Daddy-Long-Legs* by Jean Webster is the most beautiful book. Our heroine, Judy, leaves her orphanage and goes to college, funded by an unknown benefactor. A brief glimpse of him shows 'a tall, long-legged man' henceforth to be called Daddy-Long-Legs. Her letters to him (he never replies) tell of her experiences as she matures from child to young woman and it is full of tenderness and humour. No matter that it was written in 1912, it spoke to me then though it may not resonate so much with young women of today.

The school curriculum was narrow and set in stone. Every year, we read a Shakespeare play, a novel and poetry. Shakespeare lessons were enlivened by reading aloud in class. Their true drama is best appreciated when acted, not read, and luckily most (but not all) of our English teachers understood this. Many speeches from Portia in *The Tempest* to Titania in *A Midsummer Night's Dream* remain in my mind. I discovered a talent for reading aloud and I was often asked to read to the class for longer than my turn. It is a great joy, to this day, to bring stories to life for other people.

Then Poetry. I was entranced. Learning was often by rote in those days and, just like learning your times tables, it was considered beneficial to learn poems by heart. Many of my classmates hated it but I discovered something I was good at. No matter how often I felt stupid in science, was bored in geography and sadly, often history (for we were not taught about people, just events), I became alive in English and relished the sound of the words in my mouth. I learnt *The Walrus and the Carpenter* from *Alice in Wonderland* in my first year and of course knew the story from which it had come. It is complete nonsense of course and that was its attraction, leading to us reading the work of Edward Lear which I love to this day. As we grew older, the poetry we studied changed. *The Listeners* by Walter de la Mare was a wonderful poem to learn: its rhythm and strangeness held a fascination for me.

One might think that reading so much would have given me an advantage academically but, sadly, quite the reverse. I was always so wrapped up in my own world and the latest book I was reading, that I often didn't pay attention in lessons. I would gaze out of the large windows overlooking the playing fields or the quad and miss much of what I was supposed to be learning. I had many friends at school but, once I was home, and the homework was done, I would read voraciously, continuing after lights out with a torch under the bedclothes.

This was the time of the 'Angry Young Men' and, although I wasn't reading them then, many of their works were transposed to BBC dramas, much loved by my mother. From the mid-1950s to the early 1960s, they produced a body of arresting work that was grounded in the "kitchen sink" reality of working-class life and railed against the class-conscious British social order. Films such as *Look Back in*

Anger and *A Taste of Honey* reflected the alienated, rebellious, and pessimistic mood of many in post-World War Two Britain. In 1966 the BBC broadcast its gritty, realistic drama *Cathy Come Home,* a tale of homelessness which shocked the nation and brought to the fore some of the social ills facing the country. Many had previously been unaware of the gulf between what was deemed respectable and the reality of many lives. The 'Swinging 60s' had opened up society and tempted the young to rebel. Lynne Reid Banks' novel *The L Shaped Room* follows a young woman who has been turned out of her family home because she is pregnant. This was very common when it was written in 1960 and frightened many young girls like myself who read it. The advent of the contraceptive pill in the early 1960s allowed young women more sexual freedom though it horrified the older generation. It was considered a sin to have sex before marriage.

Though 'teenagers' had their own interests, culture and music, quite distinct from their parents, there was no literature written specifically for them. It was not until the 1970s that writers began targeting their books at a young adult audience. In the library, you belonged to the children's section and were not supposed to borrow from the adult library until the age of 14. By the age of 12 however, I was going alone and borrowing my mother's books for her. The librarians were quite happy to move me over. The first author I discovered there was Agatha Christie so I was kept busy reading through everything she ever wrote!

Despite the fact that I had read voraciously all my life, there were many children's classics that passed me by. My choices were pure serendipity so I missed the joy of *Narnia* and *Middle Earth* amongst others. Luckily, I caught up when

I met and married my lifetime reading partner who introduced me to many other authors. We have spent our entire lifetimes reading in bed morning and evening – I could not possibly imagine anything else!

Notes:

1 Encyclopedia Britannica online

Chapter Six
Hopscotch, Hockey & Homer

I am standing at the front of the classroom with tears in my eyes. I have been sent out to the front for talking and Mr Naish is holding the 'slipper': the black plimsoll used to beat the girls' bottoms; softer I suppose than the cane which the boys get, but still very painful. He is a very good and kind teacher and doesn't like doing it, but it is the way things are and we all know the rules. Talking in class is strictly forbidden. Eyes to the front of the class and definitely no passing notes between our single, wooden desks. I love school but often get into trouble. My enthusiasm is impossible to contain so I am regularly sent to the front for the slipper but at least I have never been sent to the headmaster, he is dreaded by us all.

I am in the top year of primary school and will be taking my Eleven Plus next year. Our classroom has a history wall along the back with all the important dates in Britain's history. I know them all and am proud to get nearly 100% in the tests. I am fascinated by the events from our past, from the Battle of Hastings in 1066 to the invention of television by John Logie Baird in 1928. There are no dates after the war, it is too recent so the history we learn stops there.

∞

I attended Richmond Road Primary School in Kingston from January 1958 until early 1964 when we moved from Kingston to Tolworth, much to my distress. I loved my school but many of the children were, according to my mother, quite 'rough', hence her deciding to send my sisters to the primary school in Latchmere Road at the 'posh' end of town. I don't remember any rough children, but I did learn to stick up for myself in the playground and was good at running away from the bigger boys. The education had not changed much in decades. Our classroom was a high ceilinged room in a large, almost prison-like building. It must have taught me well because I passed my Eleven Plus the following summer, having taken it at my new school in Tolworth, St. Matthew's. I clearly remember writing with both hands, swapping as one got tired. Though left-handed, I had been made to write with my right in my previous school so was ambidextrous. This outdated practice did not last thankfully into senior school so I soon lost that useful ability.

Richmond Road Primary School

My first day at St Matthew's sticks in my memory because of the embarrassment. I came into the classroom with the headmistress and she introduced me to the class: "This is Susan, she's very clever, you will all have to work extra hard to keep up with her." I was mortified and expected them all to hate me. Luckily for me, one girl took pity on me. Sheila was very kind and took me under her wing. I was so pleased when she too passed her Eleven Plus and the two of us went to the same grammar school. We had many teenage adventures together and have remained friends ever since. There were only three of us out of around 30 in the class who passed and one of them was given a new bicycle to celebrate. Not for me. When I suggested it to my mother, she was appalled that I might be expected to be rewarded just for being clever. It wasn't anything I'd done after all. We never talked about it in later life but I suspect she would have heartily approved of the comprehensive system, as do I.

I certainly never thought there was anything wrong. Why would I when passing the Eleven Plus was a passport to opportunity and something we all aspired to? It never occurred to me then that the other 27 children in the class were probably devastated, disappointed and, worst of all, felt they were failures. The first comprehensive had opened ten years earlier but there certainly weren't any where we lived and, indeed, Kingston held onto its grammar schools and does so until this day.

I was only at St. Matthew's a few months. In September 1964, I boarded the 406 bus at the top of Red Lion Road, changing in Kingston to the 65 bus along the Richmond Road out to Ham and the Tiffin Girls' School. I was back in Kingston and was very happy.

Tiffin Girls' School front
(Photo taken at a reunion in 2011 by which time the
School had moved to new Premises next door)

Tiffin Girls' School was founded in 1880 and its sixth headteacher, Miss Orford, had only retired the Easter before I joined the school in 1964. She had been at the school for 17 years and was much loved by the girls. Many was the time older girls would say to us "oh you should have been here with Miss Orford, we had such fun then", reacting to something the hated Miss Weedon had done or changed. Poor Miss Weedon, she was just trying to bring in more modern ideas and it was undoubtedly difficult stepping into the shoes of a much-loved, long-serving predecessor. By the time she retired in 1980 she was apparently 'much loved by both staff and students' but her early years were challenging. We knew somehow that many of the teachers found her difficult and there were many changes to the staff in my first years at the school. She certainly seemed terrifying to me and, although I luckily had few occasions to speak to her; nevertheless I never felt she was a sympathetic person, which was borne out when I left the school in 1969.

Miss Orford had made many changes to the school since the Butler Education Act of 1944 had introduced free education for all and the school was categorised as a grammar school with admission through selection. O-level and A-level qualifications were also introduced at this time and our uniform of grey skirts, blue and white blouses, blue jumpers and blazers topped by a blue beret was introduced in 1953.

Miss Weedon directed the school through much political change and the Tiffin Girls' School was one of the few schools to survive the massive drive by the Labour education policy towards comprehensive education in the 1960s and 1970s. The school continued to celebrate its birthday on 7th February but the famous birthday teas were stopped after my first year. Instead, the whole school walked into the town to see a film at the Odeon Cinema, something literary and educational of course but a great treat all the same. Just imagine, 600 girls walking down the Richmond Road in crocodile format! There was also a school assembly with a huge birthday cake and candles. Every year there was a different rule to pick the girls to light them. One year I remember it was any girl with the first or middle name of *Mary* and Sheila got to light one. I never did though I wished for it every year. At the end of the celebrations the words of our school song rang out joyfully – we really did enjoy singing it and especially the chorus:

**So we'll sing of our school
With good voice and strong
May her friends still be many
Her life full and long
And while 'neath the shade
And then on thro' the years
Let *Sapere Aude* ever ring in our ears**

Sapere Aude – Dare to be Wise – is a good school motto and has stayed with me all my life. I did not make the most of my education while I was at the school, being happy to bumble along in the middle of the class, keeping out of trouble but sometimes enjoying being friends with 'naughty' girls. However, I have been forever grateful for the confidence I gained, the belief that girls could do anything they wanted to in life and I have always been proud of the school and its traditions. It has remained a much revered and respected school and I have often impressed people when I say "I was a Tiffin girl", not just in the local area but further afield when I worked in education myself many years later.

In the summer of 1964, Mum and I made a bus trip into Kingston to visit Bentalls, the stockist for all the school uniforms in the area. The wonderland of the store was even more magical when I was whisked off by a stout lady to be fitted for the vast array of clothing I would need right down to the grey woollen PE knickers, much hated by us all. That evening I modelled my uniform for the rest of the family and was so proud and excited, I could not wait for the start of term.

Almost the first thing we were told by the older girls on arrival at the school was how to get a hopscotch pitch for break! Hopscotch was more than a passion; it was the most important part of life for the 1st and 2nd year girls. Our school was built in a rectangle, with a quad in the middle (out of bounds until the 5th year). All round the outside of the school were chalked hopscotch pitches, meaning around 30 pairs of girls could play at the same time. The fact that there were 90 girls in each year meant that only one third would get a pitch so all sorts of planning went into making sure that you were as near to an outside door as possible before the morning or lunch break. As we got older, we would even bribe a younger or less interested girl with a lesson next to a door, to 'hold a pitch for us'. The bribe would inevitably be a bun. It seemed harmless then, though unthinkable now, that buns were brought into the school every morning from the local bakers, to be sold for a penny or two. Currant buns, iced buns and jam doughnuts to keep us going until school dinner. There was never a problem of it 'spoiling your appetite', you were not allowed to leave the table until your plate was scraped clean, however much you hated what was on offer. With the bun, if you were lucky enough to have the money to buy one, was your milk. Free school milk had been provided to all children under 18 since 1946 and there was no question of not drinking it. The crates were left outside so in the winter it was ice cold and delicious. In the summer, however, it was warm and made you queasy but you had no choice but to drink it – unless of course you could somehow escape the beady eyes of the teachers on duty and pour it away somewhere! Free milk for secondary school children was stopped by Harold Wilson's government in 1968, the year before I left the school. Only a few years later, Margaret Thatcher's political career was almost derailed when she stopped free milk for over seven-year-olds, earning the epithet 'Mrs Thatcher, milk snatcher'.

Morning break and lunchtime were opportunities to get together with your friends and chat, as girls do. The grounds of the school were extensive and we were lucky to have plenty of places to sit privately with our friends. There were few rules, we were allowed to stay in the classrooms if the weather was bad, there was never any supervision and it did not seem to be a problem but then we were all expected to be 'young ladies' and most of us came up to expectation, though not all. There were two very popular outside spaces: to the left of our school was a large boys' Secondary Modern school and between the two grounds was simply a high wire fence. This was a popular place for the older girls to hang out, chatting to boys from Rivermead as long as they were not spotted by a teacher and sent away. Most of us preferred the field, a huge area the size of two hockey pitches and surrounded by trees on the other three sides. In the summer months, we would get as far away from the school buildings as we could and lie in the grass, dreaming and talking about anything and everything and wondering what we would all become. Sadly, when the school moved to the new building next door on the Rivermead site, those lovely grounds were built on and the spaciousness disappeared. It became a college so did not need playing fields but I wondered where those students could sit and dream.

Sport was important and I was lucky in that I was quite sporty though, to my disappointment, I was hopeless at tennis, despite the expensive, heavy wooden racquet I had been bought for my 11th birthday. Winter meant hockey and I was surprised to find myself picked as goalie from the very beginning. Though I was quite small, I seemed to be good at stopping goals, though maybe I was the only girl brave or stupid enough to put myself in the line of fire. We wore leg pads but no other protection but I preferred being goalie to running up and down the pitch. I was obviously reasonably good at it because in the 4th year I was picked to be goalie for the First Team, three years above me, and became part of the team touring round other schools that year. I didn't really enjoy it because, nice though they were, the girls were sixth formers and seemed so old to me, I didn't fit in. I don't know why I didn't want to run on the hockey pitch because I turned out to be a good runner in the summer athletics. Never a sprinter, but I could run long distance and by the 3rd year had made the 880 yards my speciality, representing the school at the District and County Games at Motspur Park School Games in New Malden, more than once.

Most of the day, of course, was taken up with lessons and the school day was long, starting at 8.45 am and finishing at 4 pm. Given that I had at least an hour's journey each way and then 2-3 hours homework, it was difficult to fit in anything else. The lessons you liked inevitably depended on the teacher who taught them and it was even better if you were good at those subjects. The lovely Miss Plum, our PE teacher was young and fun; Miss Cheverton, our Music teacher, was eccentric and passionate about her subject; to her I owe the discovery of Schubert's *The Trout Quintet* which is one of my favourite pieces of music to this day. That and the wonderful folk songs we used to sing: I still know all the words to *My Grandfather's Clock!* Miss Berne, our French teacher, was one of my favourites from the beginning. Despite Richmond Road Primary being a 'rough' school, I had been learning French since the age of eight so was well ahead on our arrival which helped to get into her good books. Apart from English, we studied two foreign languages. Before I started at the school, my parents had to choose between Latin and German, a strange choice seemingly between a dead language and a very modern, important one in the 1960s. I am forever grateful they chose Latin. The root of all Mediterranean languages, it has stood me in good stead all my life. It also gave me my beloved Miss Dowding. Miss Dowding was not old, but she had an aura of antiquity about her. Her greying hair resisted all attempts to keep it tidy and her scuffed shabby shoes were misshapen from her painful bunions pushing against the leather. Despite her somewhat unprofessional appearance, when she taught her subject, her passion shone through and lit her face. Her grey eyes twinkled and she rarely stopped smiling. From our very first lesson, we read Homer's *Odyssey* in Latin and I was entranced. Even more fortunate, she was our Form Mistress (no Masters in the school until 1968) in both our 1st and 5th years. She was one of the kindest people I have ever met.

Form 5B at the end of the summer term with our Form Mistress Miss Dowding

In the quad on the last day of school

Almost from the beginning, I was Peggy. In the first few days we discovered there were four Susans in the class, it being a very popular name in the 1950s and 60s. We decided between us that we would all use nicknames and these were eventually used by the teachers as well to avoid confusion. I didn't like my surname much, especially as one or two rather nasty girls somehow found out that Pegg had originally been Pigg and teased me mercilessly. My grandfather had indeed been born a Pigg but sometime in the first half of the 20th century, the family started spelling their family name as Pegg.

My father's cousin Ken had investigated the matter and received a letter from the Registrar General to say that he had been born a Pigg but that if 'you have always used and been known by the name Pegg you have acquired a right to use the name ...' In any case, I got used to being Peggy throughout my teens and the 1957 Buddy Holly song *Peggy Sue* helped!

School assembly took place every morning with every girl from the 1st to the 5th year sat on the floor in the hall, sixth formers having the privilege of chairs on the stage with the teachers. The hymns were rousing, the prayers Christian and the addresses very moral and focussed on achievement. Awards were given out every week and one of the most sought after was the 'posture star'. A throwback to the time when young ladies balanced books on their heads to make them stand up straight, these fabric stars to sew on your school jumper were surprisingly popular with the girls. Despite my mother constantly telling me I had bad posture and to stand up straight, I finally achieved one in the third year – much to her disgust.

Besides the school's birthday, there were many regular events which took place every year and one of our favourites was The Oxford and Cambridge Boat Race. This University Boat Race took place on the Thames every year and, though the first women's race took place in 1927, it was an irregular event until 1964, when it became an annual event. This was a great celebration of women's equality and was seized upon by the enthusiastic PE teachers at our all girls' school. Our race took the form of 'miles of pennies' weaving round the grounds of the school. We were allocated Oxford or Cambridge and all had to bring in pennies (the large old penny disappearing of course in 1971 with decimalisation) which were laid on the ground, the longest trail being the winner. It was a great charity fund raiser and great fun and we all loved the real race too.

School life revolves around the regularity of terms and seasons. In the Autumn term, when the nights were drawing in, our annual drama and music competitions absorbed us completely outside lesson time. Though music was not my forte, I loved being part of the drama productions and hours were spent rehearsing our plays to pit ourselves against the other forms. I have an abiding memory of playing Lady Jane Grey, the tragic 16-year-old queen who ruled for only nine days. In the Spring term we had the School Birthday and the Boat Race and, in the summer, sport and day trips and, as we got older, the chance to go away on a residential trip. In the early summer of 1968, my excitement was immense when I was allowed to join the school trip to Paris. There had been earlier trips but they were expensive and my parents could not afford to send me. No matter, the Paris trip was everything I had dreamed. We had tremendous freedom to explore on our own and discovered the fabulous shopping in the Champs Elysees and Galerie Lafayette. At night, in the dormitory of the convent school we were staying in, there was a hubbub of girls' talking well into the night and listening to the popular and exciting Radio Luxembourg, a station we could just about find in England but with very poor, crackly reception.

Although corporal punishment was still legal in English state schools and was not banned until 1987, there was very little in our school. However, one teacher, Mrs Culver, liked nothing better than to throw chalk at inattentive girls and even, on occasion, the board rubber. She was a very strict teacher and I will always remember her refusing to let me leave for a dentist appointment because she thought I wanted to get out of the lesson. I would never have had the nerve! In the main though, there were good relations between girls and staff. My favourite teachers were definitely those who taught me languages which was my strength. Along with Miss Dowding for Latin and Miss Berne for French, I met Mrs Cuthbertson when I took up German for O level in the 4th year. Because I was only to study it for two years, I was part of a group invited to her apartment after school on a regular basis for extra tuition. Much of the pleasure in those visits was undoubtedly due to the fact that her husband, Allan Cuthbertson, was a fairly famous actor at the time and we met him on more than one occasion. It was fortunate I had a talent for languages because I had none whatsoever for science. Physics and Chemistry were completely beyond me and Biology made me queasy. So I was delighted when I was allowed to give them all up at the end of the 3rd year and concentrate on the Arts, Humanities and Languages for O level. It wasn't a good decision though, my lack of basic science knowledge has been an annoyance ever since.

During my time at school, skirts became shorter and shorter. By 1966 the fashion designer, Mary Quant, had popularised the mini skirt which was six or seven inches above the knee. This was definitely not ladylike so a rule was introduced that skirts should be no more than four inches above the knee. At any time, we could be made to kneel on the floor and a teacher would take her ruler out of her pocket to check. This wasn't a problem for me. My mother hated the mini skirt and in my early years I, like many of my friends, would just roll it up from the waist so that it could easily be rolled down if you saw a teacher you thought would check.

Many of them didn't bother, they were young themselves and would probably have loved to wear them. However, by the time I reached the 3rd year, I had become more devious, swapping my long skirt for a very short one at the bus stop on my way to school! By this time, the teachers had more or less accepted the inevitable though my mother, and particularly my father, had not.

I loved school though I never really worked very hard. I was conscientious and always did my homework but I dreamed my way through much of my teens rather aimlessly. It was a huge shock to me therefore when, at 15, half-way through the 5th year, my mother decided I should leave school at the end of the year. She felt I should get a useful skill and go to secretarial college, that being an excellent and well-paid career for girls then. 'You've had enough education', she said 'it's time for you to earn a living and contribute to the household'. I could not argue, I had no idea what I wanted to do, just that I wasn't ready to leave school or to finish my education. That was one battle I was never going to win.

∞

I am standing outside Miss Weedon's office, terrified of what is to come. There are only five of us out of 90 girls who are leaving school at the end of term and we are all summoned to an interview with her. I am waiting my turn with trepidation.

'You are a disgrace to the school, Susan. Tiffin Girls do not leave in the 5th.' The tears come to my eyes; this is not my wish either. She is scathing about secretarial college. Our careers education has suggested teaching, nursing or university. Being a secretary is not something a Tiffin girl should even consider.

∞

I was determined to prove her wrong. She did me a favour in one way as it has always spurred me on to achieve. Within ten years, I had returned to study and taken English and History A levels at night-school, then later studying further by distance learning to be a librarian.

In January 1980, The Tiffin Girls' School celebrated its 100th birthday, and a Grand Reunion took place. By that time I was married with a young daughter, and meeting some of my old classmates and hearing about their achievements made me feel anew the pain of leaving school. But I realized that the most important thing was the person it had made me, the confidence and determination I had learnt was due to those teachers who made you believe you could be whatever you wanted to be in life.

Notes:

1 Kidbrooke School between Blackheath and Eltham was London's first purpose-built comprehensive opened in 1954 Family Britain p 408.

2 A Brief History of The Tiffin Girls' School – http://www.tiffingirls.org/Our-School/History.aspx accessed 14/6/20

3 The 60s mini skirt history
https://www.fashionera.com/the_1960s_mini.htm#:~:text=John%20Bates%20was%20one%20of%20the%20most%20infl

uential,least%20undergarments%20-%20he%20preferred%20a%20bra-less%20silhouette.

Chapter Seven
The Good Life

We have arrived in our new house. It seems very small to me, a much more modern, end of terrace house in a suburban street, quite unlike the spacious Edwardian rooms and huge garden of Kingston. But I am happy despite the pain of leaving, I have my own bedroom! A much longed-for and surprisingly unexpected result of our own home. It is a tiny box room with barely room to move between the wardrobe and the end of the bed, but it is my private space. Here I will dream, read and keep my secrets for most of the second decade of my life.

∞

The strangest part of moving to the house in Largewood Avenue, Tolworth was that, although we now had two living rooms instead of one, we spent almost all of our time in the kitchen/living room which was no larger than our old one in Kingston. The 'front room' was kept for best and we children rarely ventured in. Mum and Dad's friends were occasionally entertained in it but the living room, with its comfy chairs, roaring fire and bookshelves, divided from the kitchen only by a waist-high worktop was where we lived most of the time. The house was cold, heated by an open fire downstairs and a paraffin heater in the hall. Even when central heating was fitted in the mid-1960s, it was only downstairs. We still had to endure freezing cold bedrooms and I was past getting undressed in front of the fire by then.

Upstairs there were three bedrooms and a proper bathroom. Not only that, but a separate toilet too. This really was an improvement and I fully understood Mum's Saturday afternoon 'bath time' when she would lock the bathroom door, run a Fenjal bath and soak. "Go and amuse yourselves," she would say to us children.

There were other improvements: a twin tub was an early purchase, saving the many back-breaking hours washing clothes in the copper and using the mangle. It was a very noisy piece of equipment and had to be moved into the centre of the kitchen to use it, its pipes attached to the taps. It could not be left alone, when it spun the vibrations would move it across the floor so someone had to be on hand to keep it still. Even so, the time needed for the washing was probably more than halved and other tasks could be done in the kitchen while it was working, a great bonus for a busy housewife. Moving house had meant quite a lot of expense and it was now possible to buy large items on 'HP' – hire purchase. Decent people saved though, it was not quite respectable to borrow.

We had a pleasant garden, though not the wilderness of Kingston. It was much more manageable and Mum began to be a keen gardener, growing gladioli and other difficult plants as well as her beloved roses. At the bottom end of the garden was a large shed which quickly became Dad's retreat: we were all growing up and four women in the house was sometimes too much for him. There he would smoke his pipe, later cigarettes, and potter. He was a keen handyman and was always repairing or making something for the house. Even when he wasn't it was a good excuse.

From our house it was barely ten minutes' walk to Tolworth Broadway, a long, characterless road full of shops with the newly built Tolworth Tower Shopping Centre at one end. I would often be sent to do some shopping, being judged old enough at the age of 11 to manage this safely. J. Sainsbury, the grocer, was the main food shop, not a supermarket yet, it still had the separate marble counters for meat, cheese and fish. However, groceries were self-service, a real novelty and it was exciting to go down the shopping list, finding every item rather than asking for them over the counter as we had always done before. Despite having a fridge, it was still necessary to shop almost daily which was very time-consuming for housewives. All the shops closed on Wednesday afternoons and Sundays and most families probably shopped five or six times a week.

Tolworth Tower circa 1963 from the Francis Frith Collection

There were local shops at the top of our road but in winter the avenue was often flooded. We mostly only braved it on winter Sundays in our wellington boots to get our weekly sweet ration. I looked at it with jaundiced eyes, it did not feel that Tolworth was really a community and I suspect Mum felt quite isolated. The upmarket shops of Kingston were no longer a walk away but a long bus ride. Her life must have changed very much for the better when she was successful in gaining employment at Gala Cosmetics along the busy A3 within walking distance from our house. It was very exciting as they were the producer of Mary Quant cosmetics and I became the proud owner of the distinctive yellow make-up box with the white daisy logo.

To get anywhere, we had to walk up Red Lion Road to Ewell Road, an important main road from time immemorial once described as a 'narrow passage through the common lands of wild beauty'. To the east, the Ewell Road led to Ewell and Epsom, to the west to Surbiton and then Kingston. Surbiton was on two famous coaching routes to Brighton and Portsmouth and was arguably of greater importance. It was included in the Domesday Book in the Hundred of Kingston and by 1179 was mentioned as 'Subertone'. 'Taleorde', now Tolworth, was part of the manor of Long Ditton at that time. Surbiton became famous as the setting of *The Good Life*, a popular TV series of the 1970s, typifying suburban life.

Since the 1950s, the influence of television had been spreading and, much to many people's concern, encouraged an 'Americanisation' of British culture. The first commercial channel, ITV, was launched in 1955 and we were introduced to advertisements. People began to want things they didn't need, and the consumer society was born. The British, however, have always been good at laughing at themselves and the most popular TV show of the 1960s was, without doubt, the *Morecambe and Wise show*. With only three channels to watch (BBC One, BBC Two and ITV), the entire nation, or at least everyone with a television, tuned in regularly to watch Eric Morecambe and Ernie Wise and their hilarious antics, often at the expense of celebrities they invited on to their show. Less reverential but equally popular was *That Was The Week That Was,* commonly known as TW3. It broke ground in comedy by lampooning political figures and probably inspired the hugely successful satire of the 1980s *Spitting Image.* Its broadcast coincided with coverage of the Profumo affair and, for the first time, politicians and figures in authority were mocked rather than revered. More serious but also hugely popular, was the BBC's investigative programme *Panorama* launched in 1953 and continuing to this day, making it the world's longest running current affairs programme. Television brought the world into our sitting rooms and two events stand out starkly in my mind: in 1966 the dreadful disaster at Aberfan was shown on the day it happened. 144 people, mostly children, died when the slurry from the coalmine above the town, cascaded down the hill, destroying everything in its path and smothering the children sitting in their school classrooms. The shock to the nation was immense and made a huge impression on me. I was not much older than the children who died and it awoke a fierce sense of unfairness. My mother's working-class roots meant she too felt that strongly. The tragedy should never have happened. Residents and local officials had raised concerns with the National Coal Board about the heap of waste located above the local primary school, but they were ignored. The implication was the miners should not make a fuss or the mine would close. In complete contrast, the Apollo Moon landings in the summer of 1969 were incredibly exciting. It seemed that the possibilities of technology were unlimited and could only improve all our lives. Television was showing us a changing world, one that seemed to promise much. As Harold Wilson said, in 1963 "The Britain that is going to be forged in the white heat of this revolution will be no place for restrictive practices or for outdated methods on either side of industry ..." Sadly, this proved to be prescient of what was to come. The bitter wars between government and unions in the ensuing decades resulted in the decline of Britain's manufacturing base and a continuation of the gap between the working classes and the increasingly affluent and growing white collar middle classes.

Meanwhile, our family was neither. Despite our move to suburbia, Mum referred to us as lower middle class, no doubt in her eyes a step up from working class. She certainly did not want to be thought of as middle class like her parents-in-law, feeling somehow that their sense of entitlement was not something she wanted to emulate. She did, however, very much enjoy having a house of their own and some of the trappings of middle-class life they could now enjoy. One of the first additions to the home was the black Bakelite telephone, sat proudly on the hall table, with its number clearly displayed in the middle of the dial: Lower Hook 2529. Telephone numbers were a lot shorter then.

It was supposed to be for emergencies, telephone calls were expensive, so it wasn't long before I had to pay for my long telephone calls with friends, sitting on the stairs in the freezing cold but very much enjoying the connections with friends even when I couldn't be with them. How much easier social media makes the lives of teenagers now!

My first friends in our new life were the Nicholsons who lived at number 12. Linda, just a year younger than me, and her little sister Marion, were the daughters of an enthusiastic and caring man who was Sunday School Superintendent at the Methodist Church on Surbiton Hill. Meeting the Nicholsons changed my life. Surbiton Hill Methodist Church was a huge community, offering not only church and Sunday School but also its own tennis club, drama group and youth club. There I met some of the most important people in my life, many of whom were mentors and good friends in my troubled teenage years.

Photo: Surbiton Hill Methodist Church

Intense Methodist activity in the area in the second half of the 19th century resulted in land being purchased for the building of a new Chapel at Surbiton Hill. The site was first fenced and let for grazing while money was raised by subscription for its building, returning to the local people the original use of the land. The foundation stone was laid in September 1881 and the church opened for worship in May 1882. An interesting book on the history of the church shows that many generations of the same families had been, and were still in the 1960s, connected to 'The Chapel on the Hill'. In 1967 major renovation and development took place to meet the needs of the increasing youth work. This was the emerging era of 'the teenager'. Young people had more freedom and independence and wanted places to go. The church filled a real need in the area and young people came from miles around to attend the twice weekly youth club. It even had its own dedicated space with a coffee bar. The 'Hubbub Club' attracted boys and girls right up to the age of 17 or 18. Even when we were old enough to meet at the pub, the youth club still had a place in our social life.

By the mid-1960s, the church was a large part of my life. From attending the senior Sunday school, I very soon started helping out with the primary children, something I loved doing and continued to do for many years, continuing after I had my own children and moved away from the area. The lovely ladies who ran the department were Ruth and Jeannette and they were very kind to me, often advising and listening to my troubles. They seemed old but of course they were young themselves, just a few years older than me with young families. Other teenagers helped out too and there I met the first love of my life. Ken was two or three years older, good looking in a babyface sort of way, great fun and a huge fan of Crystal Palace football club. This was the beginning of many emotional ups and downs but also a great friendship with his whole family.

Bob Nicholson was also a great dramatist and enjoyed putting on huge productions which included all the children in Sunday school, often as many as 40 or 50. My first appearance was in *Hans Christian Andersen* in 1968, a play Bob wrote himself featuring many of the famous stories. My part was to introduce the play by reading the stories to my little sisters – played by my real sisters. Because I was to be in contemporary dress and have no costume, I was allocated a budget to buy a new dress. Not just any dress, but a really modern one which Mum and I went to Carnaby Street to buy. I am not sure that my psychedelic orange and yellow dress suited me but it certainly was modern!

Cast of Hans Christian Andersen at the presentation of a cheque to Lady Mary Hoare, founder of a charitable trust to raise money for the families of Thalidomide children.

The Boyfriend and *Salad Days* followed in 1969 and 1970 but though I longed for a big part, I was only ever a bit player, unlike at school where I often had leading roles. Not that it mattered, it was such huge fun being part of the large cast, rehearsing for many months and making lasting friendships. This was the time when I became friends with Ken's sister, Heather, and Janet Teare as she was then. Janet was also at Tiffins but the year below me so we had not met at school. We three were regular members of the youth club and drama group and became firm friends, holidaying together in later years and supporting each other in the tragedy that followed in the summer of 1972. Janet and I spent many teenage hours together and had a great foursome with Ken and his friend John. They weren't really our boyfriends, just boys to hang out with though I suspect we would both have liked them to be. Janet was one of the few girls who went away to university but we kept in touch and have remained friends all our lives. Her life was different to mine and so too was her mother, a successful and very kind lady who gave me much good advice and a refuge when I needed it. In the late 60s and early 70s, just over half a million young people went to university as opposed to around two million today. For most girls, their ambition was to earn a bit of money, then get married and have a family, probably not working while they brought up their children. I wanted to marry one day but I was ambitious and wanted to do something with my life. The trouble was, I didn't know what and when it came to arguing with my mother about leaving school in 1969 I couldn't say why I should stay on. I just knew I loved reading and studying and wasn't ready to grow up.

Photo: Surbiton Hill Library

Just a few steps further up the hill from the church was my other haven – Surbiton public library. As soon as we moved to Tolworth, we joined the library on the hill, there was no library in Tolworth. Mum joined but rarely visited, it was quite a chore to get the twins ready and walk a good half an hour to the library, and then not to be able to browse in peace. Very quickly, I was deputised to get books for her. Armed with a list of favourite authors, I would browse myself but also get help from the kindly librarian. Choosing Mum's books and my own took time and I spent many happy hours in the quiet stacks. Built in 1932, the library was a beautiful brick building with gleaming wood floors and shelves and it became my gateway to the world. Within a year, I had outgrown the children's section and was allowed, two years early, to progress to the adult library. There were no book lists or suggestions then resulting in the joy of serendipity as I browsed the shelves. There were always well informed and patient librarians to make suggestions but I was never told a book wasn't suitable or I wouldn't like it. Walking home with a bag full of books, I would dream of working in a bookshop, though never, strangely enough, of being a librarian which I became many years later. Surbiton Library is still beautiful, even more so now its dark shelving has been removed and space given over for students to study, but it cannot mean more to them than it did to me then. One beautiful addition is an ornate plaque to Alfred Bestall, famous writer and illustrator of Rupert the Bear, a popular comic strip in the Daily Express for many years. He too was a member of the Methodist church though I never knew him.

To the east of Surbiton Hill was the suburban area known as Berrylands. With its wide avenues and large houses, it was very middle class and home to many London commuters. The fast train to London Waterloo from Surbiton Station took only 16 minutes and many professionals found it a very convenient place to live. Berrylands had its own station, though on the slow service, situated conveniently next to The Berrylands pub, where I worked evening shifts in later years. Most of my friends lived in Berrylands so I spent a lot of time there. I spent less and less time at home but sadly I was welcome at my friends' houses whilst they were not welcome at mine. With the benefit of hindsight, I think Mum was threatened by my middle-class friends and did not want to be looked down on.

Despite becoming a teenager in the 'Swinging Sixties', a lot of it passed me by though by 1970 when I went to college, I became more a part of the revolution that was occurring. It was a time of great change when young people began to want their independence before they left home. The trouble was some parents, and most definitely mine, did not welcome the change. Their parents had ruled the roost and they expected to – they were always right no matter how old you were! I did not see myself as a rebel but I was, and am, strong-minded and independent. I did not realise then but I was just like my mother really. The difference was that I had the opportunities she did not. It is sad that she resented that but now I realise that she was not really happy with her own life.

∞

Disaster has struck! Dad was found by the police sleeping in the car on his way home from a late music night. He was made to take the new breathalyser to measure alcohol in the blood and is going to lose his driving licence. Mum is furious. She relies on him to go anywhere apart from work, which she can walk to. She will be even more trapped and, for once, I look beyond myself and feel really sorry for her.

∞

I can imagine the shame my mother must have felt at the time but, in fact, it spurred her on to learn to drive. We learnt the same year and the freedom it gave her improved her life immeasurably. Her green Standard 10 sat proudly in the road and she became a happier person. Though we still argued, the balance was shifting. I was contributing to the household by handing over some of my wages and would not always do as I was told.

Notes:

1 Fenjal bath products were an expensive treat so a great idea for birthday and Christmas presents for Mum!

2 Profumo Affair – a political scandal regarding a sexual relationship between John Profumo, the Secretary of State for War in Harold Macmillan's government, and Christine Keeler, a 19 year old model.

3 Aberfan Disaster – History.com

4 Chapel on the Hill by Pendry Morris 1982 (Chapel on the Hill by Pendry Morris (Liz's Dad) is dedicated to Philip Turner (Arthur's Dad)

5 Carnaby Street in London's West End is commonly accepted to be the birthplace of the 'Swinging Sixties', the fashion capital of the world at the time

6 1970 vs 2010: 40 years when we got older, richer and fatter | The Independent

Chapter Eight
Playtime

We are so proud of our new hats! Our jingle has won runner-up in the Heinz Beanz competition and the money has bought us all one of the new berets for our Girls' Brigade uniform. I love Monday evenings at the Baptist church where our two jolly leaders arrange an evening of working for badges and having fun. I want to go to camp in the summer but I am not sure Mum will let me. It will cost quite a lot and there is not much money to spare. The Captain and the Lieutenant have offered to help pay for me and Mum is very cross with me for telling them we can't afford it.

∞

I joined the Girls' Brigade in 1964, soon after we moved to Tolworth. It was very exciting to be out on my own in the evening. Apart from travelling to school and back in the dark winter mornings and evenings, I did not go out after dark. Most of my school friends lived too far away although I often went to Sheila's house after school. The Girls' Brigade is a Christian organization for girls, similar to the Brownies and

Guides, though with more of a military feel: even the leaders were called Captain and Lieutenant and there was a lot of marching and singing hymns. Church Parade one Sunday a month was more or less compulsory but that was no hardship. We would join all the Guides, Brownies, Scouts, Cubs and Boys' Brigade members at the church whose turn it was to host this huge gathering of young people. More people went to church and Sunday school regularly then so it wasn't unusual. In fact, there was very little else to do on a Sunday. Everything was shut and Sunday was still considered a day of rest when families were together. For many non-church-going parents, Sunday school was a way of getting rid of the children for a couple of hours. At least we only went once on a Sunday. When we went down to our cousins in Southsea, we had to go in the afternoon as well!

The Girls' Brigade encouraged my sense of independence when I went to camp, my first holiday away on my own. I cried inconsolably on my return. I didn't want to come home but it wasn't surprising. To be away with friends and away from the family was a new experience for me. Our leaders were ambitious for us and we regularly entered competitions such as the Heinz Beanz jingle. We were active too, winning through to the final rounds of a synchronized exercise competition to appear in the 1967 Rally and Display at the Royal Albert Hall, my first experience of what has become one of my favourite places. The excitement and pride at performing on its magic circular floor was immense.

Photo: Programme for the 1967 Rally

∞

Although by the mid-60s most households had a television, the lure of 'the pictures' was unbeatable. There were cinemas in nearly every town. Tolworth did not have its own but Surbiton Odeon was a short bus ride away. 'Saturday Morning Pictures' was attended by thousands of children across the country. From the age of 5, children would be treated to films specially commissioned, featuring well-known names such as Laurel & Hardy, Old Mother Reilly and the beautiful child star, Shirley Temple. Parents did not attend; the supervision was done by cinema staff and older children. So on a Saturday morning, I would take my sisters out for the morning and we would love the freedom of it. I began to see them as real people instead of the babies they had been before. Hardly babies, they were 6 when we moved house but it was the first time we had fun together. As we got older, the cinema continued to be something we enjoyed together, particularly the musicals that were becoming popular. We knew all the songs from *The Sound of Music* and *Mary Poppins* and sang them incessantly, particularly on long car journeys.

Later Saturdays came to mean football. My crush on Ken inevitably meant I became interested in his club, Crystal Palace. Ken's whole family were huge football and Crystal Palace fans and I was soon going along to home matches and the occasional away game. I did not have to fake the interest. At my first home game I was converted. England had won the World Cup the previous year and the whole country was football mad. Crystal Palace were in Division Two and were always being promoted or relegated but it did not matter at all. The team were all local lads and we felt we knew them all. The atmosphere in the stands was friendly and jolly and we were drunk with the excitement of it all. The crowd was mostly men and boys but Heather, Ken's sister, and I shouted and screamed as loud as any of them.

My other sporting passion was tennis, one I shared with my mother. Wimbledon fortnight in our house was sacrosanct. Every afternoon, I would get home from school to find Mum glued to the black and white television screen. Tea would be delayed if a match was at a crucial point although coverage of the play stopped in the early evening. After all, women would need to get their husband's dinner on the table. The middle Saturday was a day when we would all sit down and watch, even Dad occasionally, though he was more a player of the game than a watcher. This was before the open era, when tennis became a professional game. The amateurs were gentlemen and ladies, almost from a bygone age: our favourite players were John Newcombe, Rod Laver, Tony Roche and, in the ladies, the British Ann Jones and Virginia Wade. We were lucky that our church had its own tennis club though, unfortunately, I was never any good at the game I loved so much. It did have the benefit though of adding to my social life and an opportunity to 'ballboy' at the Surrey Championships held at Surbiton Tennis Club before the open era. Considered an important warm-up event for Wimbledon, it attracted big stars and my first match was for Scottish player, Winnie Shaw who went on to reach the Wimbledon semi-finals a few years later. Janet was a good tennis player and we spent many good summer evenings at our club, playing but also socializing with others from the church and youth club.

Summer also meant visits to the open-air swimming pool in Berrylands. Surbiton Lagoon, like many other lidos at the time, was the meeting hub for young people during the summer months. According to records, the summers of the 1960s were not particularly good but, in my memory they are, of course, full of sunshine and lazy days. There must have been some good days because it was not unusual to walk home avoiding the hot tarmac melting on the pavement. The long summer evenings and the hot days of the school holidays were perfect opportunities to head for the Lagoon with friends, to lie around on the hot concrete, avoiding the mothers and children on the grass, to splash in the fountains, dive from the high boards and hurtle into the water from the breath-taking waterslide. The queues at the turnstiles were always long but somehow, once inside, there was plenty of room for everyone. The huge pools attracted people from miles around and had done since it was built in 1934. Its popularity was sadly brief. It closed in 1979 for essential repairs and never re-opened.

Photos of Surbiton Lagoon from the Francis Frith collection

∞

Methodism had become a huge and very important part of my life. Of course, religion was very much more part of everyone's life. Daily Christian assemblies took place at every school, most children attended Sunday school and a Christian organization such as Guiding, Scouting or the Brigades. We learnt the Lord's Prayer as very young children, whether or not your parents went to church. We sang hymns daily except for Saturday, in school assemblies Monday to

Friday and in church on Sunday. Even so, Methodism was more modern in its outlook. The Wesleyan hymns were familiar from my Granny Stillwell and there was no mass or Latin to deal with. Methodism has always had a great tradition of youth work and Surbiton Hill was a shining example. What young person would not be attracted by a twice-weekly youth club, a drama club, badminton club and its own tennis club. Attending church once a week was a price worth paying even for those who did not want to! Some of those teenagers coming from further afield were from Kingston Methodist which I had attended as a child. Imagine my delight when I met friends from my early years and became friends once again. In particular, the Daniel brothers, Rob and Andy, and the Jones brothers, Gareth (Gaz) and Jonah (I have no recollection of his real name!) became firm friends and part of a great gang over the next few years.

Our church youth club was part of MAYC, the Methodist Association of Youth Clubs, a huge, nationwide organization of clubs which arranged many inter-club events. The annual rally at the Royal Albert Hall would see thousands of young people from all over the country sporting the trademark yellow and green scarves, and probably imaginative clothing in the same colours, all converging on the Albert Hall for the rally and service. The circular corridors rang with laughter and recognition as we met friends from previous years and weekends together. For, as well as the annual London Weekend, every club had a weekend partner. Our whole club would travel by coach to another; sleep on their church hall floors and take part in a fantastic programme of activities they had arranged. We were the London hosts, our partners were at Eastbourne by the sea, and each club loved the visits to the other. Many young people would have no other holidays. Lasting friendships and even marriages were made in those youthful heady days. As I grew older, I helped to run events for the younger members including leading a netball team. To my shame I still remember getting them lost on the way to a tournament! Years later as an adult, I helped to run an MAYC club. Attending the London weekend in the spring of 1995, it seemed almost unchanged. The passion and excitement of the young people was just the same.

Another great example of Methodism's youth work was its Guild Holiday Homes. All over the country, holiday homes ensured a safe way for teenagers to holiday without their parents, though many families stayed too. In the summer of 1970, when I was still just 16, my friend Sue Meads and I took the train to Eastbourne and our first holiday on our own. Sue was one of the four Susans in my class at school, known as 'Specs' (she wore glasses) and we had become good friends during long, hot summers at Surbiton Lagoon. The Home was a large old manor house, set in the wide, tree-lined streets of Eastbourne behind the coast road. The rooms were comfortable, the people friendly and the weather hot: we were set for a wonderful week. This was not to be: on our first day we spent far too long at the beach (no parents to advise us of course!) and arrived back at the Home very tired and sunburnt. Within hours, Sue was taken very ill with sunstroke and her parents came to take her home. I was devastated and rang home to ask Mum what I should do. To her credit, she said not to spoil my holiday but, instead, to ask my boyfriend down for the rest of the week. Andy and I had been dating for some months so I rang him from the phone box in the hall and with the help of the kindly housemother, arranged a room for him to stay in the nearby village.

The train from London pulled into Eastbourne station and Andy jumped down from the train with his trademark boyish grin and his long hair flopping over his eyes. We walked along the promenade – and walked. Something was wrong, normally we could chat away for hours and were more like best friends than boyfriend and girlfriend but there were long silences and he would not meet my eye. Eventually I made him tell me. In my absence, he had started dating one of my best friends! I had met Miki (Michelle) at Kingston College of Further Education. She was in the secretarial course with Sheila and I and other friends from school and we had all become good friends and part of the same gang that hung out at the Glyn Arms in Ewell. Strangely enough, it did not break up my friendship with either her or Andy. I knew that I was not in love with him so could not be jealous. It didn't last. A few months later Andy and I were back together for another two years.

But that summer afternoon, it was a different story. I was furious and insisted on him catching the next train home. Despite his pleading that I would spoil my holiday, I was adamant. I watched the train pull out and walked slowly back to the Home. Despite the inauspicious start, I had a wonderful week. The home was full of young people and they took me under their wing. I had proved my resilience and was proud of myself. From that time on, I knew I could stand on my own two feet.

∞

I have been blessed with many good friends in my life and in those teenage years they were my lifeline. Whatever was happening at home, my friends were always there for me, and many still are to this day. The 1960s saw the blossoming of young people's independence and, for the first time, it was possible to be friends with boys as well as girls. Our large overlapping group included those from Kingston, Surbiton and then further afield to Epsom and Ewell. Many of the boys began to drive and some had cars or motorbikes. Hordes of us would go swimming in the river on Sunday afternoons or head to the Glyn Arms pub in Ewell on a Friday and Saturday nights for darts and bar billiards. Sunday evening was youth club. Although pubs were open on a Sunday evening, most parents would have been horrified if we had gone to the pub on a Sunday.

The summer after the fateful Eastbourne holiday was in complete contrast. The age of package holidays had begun and Janet, Heather, Kate and I set off to Majorca. The age of majority had been reduced from 21 to 18 the previous year and we were all about to become adults. My 18th birthday was spent on that sun-kissed island, celebrating with bubbly and great friends. I felt that life was finally beginning.

Chapter Nine
I Heard It Through
the Grapevine

Sheila and I are sitting in her bedroom. There are records all over the bed. Mostly singles but she has a few LPs of which I am very jealous. Her brother, Howard, plays the guitar and buys lots of records so she knows a lot more about music than me. Howard likes heavier music so we listen to *The Who, Led Zeppelin and Pink Floyd.* My tastes are lighter but certainly much more modern than the music of Mum and Dad which seems very old fashioned. I love coming to Sheila's for tea after school. Her Mum and Dad are older than mine but so kind, both with a twinkle in their eye and they treat me like a daughter. Sheila is the much-loved youngest child so her family feels very different to mine.

∞

Sheila and I met at primary school in 1964. We both passed our Eleven Plus that summer and opted to go to the grammar school in Kingston, Tiffin Girls. For the next five years, we boarded the bus at the top of Red Lion Road and travelled to school together. We continued to take more or less the same journey when we both left school in 1969 and attended KCFE, Kingston College of Further Education, to take our Secretarial course, two of those five 'failures' according to Miss Weedon, our Headmistress. Sheila was my best friend and, though we both had other friends at school, we were partners in crime in many ways and she was my rock through our teenage years. Her parents were far more easy-going than mine and she seemed to have a lot more freedom. Her house was always open to me and we would often go back after school for tea and chat, doing our homework together and listening to music.

The music scene was changing rapidly and was very exciting for teenagers. The jazz scene that Dad was part of was all I knew and any music we listened to was via the radio. Mum listened to the Light programme (which became Radio 2) which played all the popular 'housewives' favourites' like Tony Bennett, Acker Bilk and Ella Fitzgerald. Although rock musicians were becoming well known, they were not tolerated in our house. Dad thought most modern music was rubbish! In 1963, when the Beatles appeared on *Sunday Night at the London Palladium,* Dad dismissed them as 'a flash in the pan'.

In the mid-1960s Mum and Dad bought a record player and what delight it was to be able to buy records for ourselves. My first single was *Concrete and Clay* by Unit 4 + 2 but more important was my first LP, *Reach Out* by the Four Tops, which started a passion for Tamla Motown, an important factor in my eventual marriage! From 1963 until December 1966 *Ready, Steady, Go* was shown on commercial television featuring the latest pop records but the BBC's *Juke Box Jury* was more popular in our house with the host David Jacobs declaring a Hit or a Miss with his famous hooter. Also popular in most households with a television was *Top of the Pops* which was to become the longest running music show, its last episode appearing in July 2006. Rather than just playing the music, TOTP as it became known, actually had the bands performing live. Many of their careers were made by their appearances on the show. A new glamorous world was opening up to us and Mum began to love the new pop music as much as I did though Dad never got used to it.

On Sunday nights, the radio featured the Top 20 hits and I would listen in my bedroom, avidly listening and trying to do my homework at the same time. Radio 1 had started in 1967 and at last it felt as though there was a real home for teenagers, Radio 2 becoming more middle of the road. The television had to be shared with the family but I soon had my own transistor radio which I could listen to in my bedroom, it felt like the height of sophistication. Another popular radio station, though not one most of us could get on our radios, was Radio Luxembourg. Luxembourg 208 was the biggest commercial radio station in Europe and had a huge influence on generations of listeners. On my only school trip abroad, to Paris in 1968, what delight it was to tune in and hear everything with absolute clarity, none of the hiss and crackle that we were used to at home. A dormitory of girls was in heaven.

Music formed the backdrop to a new generation, flexing their muscles and pushing boundaries. HMV record stores became the place to visit on Saturday afternoons. We could never buy as much as we wanted so the next best thing was to visit the popular Wimpy Bar where we could insert a coin into the juke box and get three popular songs. Wimpy was American, so it was ultra-sophisticated to us, as was buying a cup of coffee – most people only drank tea.

Youth clubs also became a great place to share music. Most churches offered youth groups but they had formerly been organized activities. With the advent of pop music, teenagers were quite happy to sit around and chat, listening to pop records they all brought to share. It was still a novelty to be able to chat to boys. Not long ago, we would have had to go to a dance and wait to be asked. I only had one experience of such a dance at the Surbiton Assembly Rooms where the boys lined one side of the hall and the girls the other. I never went again, though I think they had fallen out of fashion anyway by the mid-1960s, the organization of the dancing probably not having changed since the time of Jane Austen! Until the 1960s everyone learnt ballroom dancing but my limited skills learnt at the ABC School of Dancing above the Odeon Cinema in Kingston were not put too much use. Instead, we began to copy the Americans and try to jive or rock and roll, both of which, quite quickly became old-fashioned and replaced with the rather shapeless jigging around which was all our less rhythmic, new music allowed. The Odeon was also used for concerts though my parents were not keen for me to go to these hotbeds of vice so the only one I attended was to see The Herd with heart-throb Peter Frampton as the lead singer. I didn't really enjoy it, you couldn't hear the music for all the girls screaming and it seemed rather pointless to me.

One of the first youth clubs I attended was the 'Young Congs' at the Congregational Church in Kingston, boarding the bus in the evening, in itself rather daring. The bare church hall was transformed with low lighting and the record player worked tirelessly to produce a heady atmosphere for boys and girls to mingle and get to know each other. It was there I first heard the song *Peggy Sue* by Buddy Holly though it had been released in 1957. It was played as a joke by one of the boys who found out my nickname but I secretly rather liked it.

But it was the Hubbub Club at Surbiton Hill Methodist that became my home from home and, unfortunately, the cause of much conflict between my mother and I. The club met on Fridays and Sundays and as Sunday was the only night my parents socialized, I was often required to babysit. I didn't have a choice but that didn't stop me complaining regularly which seems in hindsight quite selfish now but then I felt I was missing out dreadfully. By the late 1960s, young people had become much more independent and the generation gap between them and their parents was almost a chasm. Life for our parents had not changed much from the generation before but, for us, the world was a completely different place with opportunities opening up all around us. The Hubbub Club had its own room with a coffee bar and record player and it was there I developed my musical tastes and made many friends. Many of the songs became a soundtrack to my life and still remind me of relationships and golden moments. One such is *Albatross* by Fleetwood Mac, a band I have loved ever since. Indeed, they became one of the world's best-selling bands and continued to contribute to the soundtrack of my life– not least with *The Chain,* the theme tune for Formula One Motor Racing, loved by my husband and later my son.

Tamla Motown music began to feature heavily. *I heard it through the grapevine* by Marvin Gaye was released in late 1968 and went straight to the top of the charts. We loved it and all the other soul music which was becoming so popular. Artists such as Diana Ross and the Supremes, Stevie Wonder, the Temptations and many more were so different to the crooners of our parents' generation, the depth of their voices and the hint of sex made it seem exciting and forbidden.

With Fridays and hopefully Sundays organized, Saturday became the night we had to find something to do. There were regular house parties amongst our crowd of friends which all blur in my memory to a lot of alcohol and many tears. My mid-teens were marked by my enduring crush on Ken and I would spend many hours crying in a friend's arms while I watched him with another girl. Looking back, I blush to think of how I threw myself at him and was always available should he look my way. There were Saturday nights when he and his friend John would ask Janet and I whether we wanted to go out and I hoped against hope it meant something though I knew in my heart it never did. I could never hear the song *Love is All Around* by The Troggs without squirming with embarrassment.

Winter evenings would always be at the church but often in the summer months there would be discos at the church tennis club. Despite it being the same crowd, somehow the dynamics were different and there were many golden evenings. Perhaps it was because we had all became such close friends and were comfortable with each other, but I do not remember the feelings of angst that were common to me at the Hubbub coffee bar. Indeed, even the music was kind. Simon and Garfunkel had become one of our most favoured bands and *Scarborough Fair* was regularly played. The film *The Graduate* with Dustin Hoffman became a huge hit for its rather daring portrayal of a young man being seduced by an older woman, and Simon and Garfunkel's *Mrs Robinson* as its theme song added to its allure. When *Bridge over Troubled Water* was released in 1970, it instantly became my favourite album and remains one even now. With its mixture of sad, thoughtful and upbeat tracks, there was something for every mood.

The summer *Bridge over Troubled Water* was released, Sheila came to stay when the rest of my family went on holiday. This had become an annual event which we loved. By the time I was 16, they were prepared to leave me at home as long as I was not on my own. Better no doubt than dragging along a grumpy teenager. One of the only tasks we had to fulfil while my parents were away was, rather strangely, to keep the fire going. The Baxi burner in our front room heated the hot water for the house so it had to stay alight all year round. It was challenging and we frequently struggled to keep it alight. But because we were young and had our freedom, we could not be serious. The fire was named *Cecilia* for the song lyrics – *you're breaking my heart, you're shakin' my confidence daily!* It was silly but we laughed so much.

The summer of 1971 was probably no better weather than most English summers but, in my memory, the days were warm and sunny and, more importantly, the nights were balmy. Sheila and I were dating two brothers – Rob and Andy (the very same who had let me down the year before). They lived in Kingston, only half an hour or so away on the bus and we would regularly go over to spend the evenings with them. However, my parents were away and Rob and Andy's parents were not about to spoil our fun so we stayed far longer than we should have and regularly missed the last bus home. It was two hours' walk home but we didn't mind, even when we were stopped by the local police in the early hours. Two young ladies out so late was unusual and this was the second night they had seen us. That wasn't the only time I was out late knowing my parents would not have approved but it was probably the first.

∞

Though I later regretted leaving school in the fifth, starting college was very exciting. I had been earning money at my Saturday job and now I would no longer be wearing school uniform, I needed more clothes. No more Marks & Spencer for me. Now I could choose my own, the more modern and cheaper, styles on offer at C&A were more attractive. Skirts were either very long or very short, a fashion abhorred by parents. My father was horrified at the length of my skirts and I often had to sneak out with a longer coat covering me so that he did not make me change. Hot pants were even worse though actually more modest. The rise of the mini skirt led to the availability of tights which protected our modesty. At school, in the fifth form, we were still wearing socks, or stockings with a suspender!

There were other girls from my school who were on the same secretarial course as Sheila and I and we soon formed a tight knit group who socialized and shared much together. No more school dinners, we could buy snacks from the café and we would sit in the common room sharing our No.6 cigarettes and listening to Black Sabbath, a new band often cited as pioneering heavy metal music.

As we grew older, visits to the Glyn Arms in Ewell began to replace youth club evenings. It was a great place for young people with the 'barn bar' given over to bar billiards, darts and the very first electronic tennis game. They were great evenings with a mix of young people from far and wide so I began to meet other boys including two lovely lads from Sutton, Matthew and his friend Richard Williams, known as Will. Many of the boys now had cars so you could always get a lift there and back. Unbelievably though, I had to get the bus home late at night. My curfew was 11 pm, the time the pub closed. I could easily have got a lift and been home by 11.30 but Mum was having none of that. 11 o'clock, no matter that I had to stand at a dark bus stop on my own. It was understandable in some ways as she would not go to sleep until I was home but it still seems like madness. She did not know, of course, that I had once got into a stranger's car and had a lucky escape. I never told her, being more frightened of her than what had nearly happened!

Of course, the barn bar had a juke box and the music now began to feature individual Beatles. The world-famous band had split up in 1969 and each began to go their own way and make individual records. Among the most popular of that time were *My Sweet Lord* by George Harrison and *Imagine* by John Lennon. Paul McCartney had formed the band Wings and their music was regularly played though, interestingly, not bought by most of us. We were exploring music other than the most popular.

We didn't often have a chance to hear live music but by 1970, our local pub in Surbiton, The Berrylands, began to feature a young band, one of whom was the son of the landlord. Phil and Larry played every Sunday evening and soon drew a large crowd of young fans. Another great meeting place was born and Sundays became the 'Berry night'. They were good and sang great covers of, amongst others, the Mamas and the Papas. *California Dreaming* became their signature tune and still reminds me of those wonderful evenings decades later. Occasionally, they would invite a contribution from the audience. Our friend John had a wonderful voice and his rendition of *My Way* was superb. The song still brings tears to my eyes to this day.

It was at the Berrylands that I got to know Matthew better. By the time I finally broke off my relationship with Andy in early 1972, we had become good friends. Matthew and Will frequented the Toby Jug and the Tolworth Bowl on Friday nights and invited me along. There was a very popular disco with a famous DJ and a huge crowd took part in line dancing (mostly the boys!). It became a regular weekly event as Matthew and I began seriously dating and I realized I was growing up – no longer troubled with teenage crushes but slowly falling in love to a soundtrack that included *American Pie* by Don Maclean, *Nights in White Satin* by The Moody Blues and *Rocket Man* by Elton John amongst many others.

And then the music died.

These words from the song *American Pie* came to signify for me the shattering events of late August 1972. Four beautiful young men, all 22 and with successful jobs and great futures, went out in a boat on a calm, summer's day and never returned. Ken, John, Paul and Mick were all part of our wide network of friends and popular with everyone. Their deaths ripped us apart. The search and then funerals and memorials seemed a blur and we were shocked and unbelieving that such a thing could happen. There was never an explanation and only three of them were found, but none of them will ever be forgotten. Although initially, we grieved together, it was the end of our happy gang of friends. People went away to university, moved away from home and tried to get on with their lives. Being with others of the gang was too painful and, in any case, we were all grown up and going our separate ways.

Chapter Ten
A Working Girl

I am sitting in the launderette, a warm and steamy place. It is full of women watching their washing go round in the huge laundromat machines. Many households do not have a washing machine so my mother is lucky that she does not have to spend her time here. I am not here for our washing but for Mr Wilson's. Today he has given me a book of poetry and I am engrossed in it. I love coming here with my book to escape our busy home.

∞

It does not seem like much of a job now but it was my first taste of independence and Mr Wilson was a kind man. He had advertised in a shop window for someone to take his washing to the launderette on a weekly basis, he was old and did not like going out, particularly to a launderette full of women. My mother came with me to check on him but she need not have worried, he was an ex-teacher and talked to me about many things when I called to collect and deliver his washing. His gift of *Summoned by Bells* by John Betjeman, which he gave me when I left his employment, was, and still is, a treasured book, building on my love of poetry which I was discovering at school. I cannot remember how much I was paid but it was my first taste of my own money and I was able to buy singles, magazines and stockings from Woolworth's on my regular after school visits with Sheila. I was 14. As my mother pointed out to me, the age at which she had left school and started contributing to the family purse.

It was certainly better paid pro rata than my next job at the Tolworth Bakery on The Broadway. It was hard work, standing on my feet from 9 in the morning until 4 or 5 in the afternoon but we were rewarded with leftover buns to take home. I wasn't keen though on the hairnets we had to wear behind the counter, though looking back, it was more hygienic than many shops now. It was busy so the time went very quickly but there were only a few girls. I could not wait until I was 15 and could get a job at one of the chain stores in Kingston. Not only were they much more glamorous, but there were hordes of Saturday staff, girls and boys, we had regular breaks and the chance at lunchtime to go shopping.

I spent nearly two years working at Littlewoods in Kingston High Street, working my way up from an assistant on the men's trousers counter (I had a spotty boy with me to measure the inside leg of the customers!) to a supervisor in the men's section. I had no intention of a career in retail but I was good at talking to customers and reasonably confident. Surprisingly, I also found I was better at the maths than many of the other Saturday staff. It was simple arithmetic really but I had been shopping for Mum for years so it came naturally to me. Everyone paid in cash then, even for expensive items such as clothing. You needed to be able to work out how much change to give, the till did not do it for you. As a supervisor, I had to bag up the money at the end of the day and it had to tally exactly. It was collected by the Accounts staff in bags of copper, silver and notes: we were still using 'old money' which included 10 shilling and £1 notes. I had left by the time decimalization occurred in 1971.

It was exciting to have money to buy my own clothes but I had to save. I was giving a third of my salary (5 shillings – 25p in today's money) to my mother which I wasn't too happy with but she was following the same pattern as that of her mother before the war: going out to work meant more money for the household. Life in the 60s had changed a great deal, but not that much as far as my mother was concerned.

I carried on working at Littlewoods all through my time at Kingston College of Further Education. In the late 1960s being a secretary was considered a very good job, with good prospects and salaries. Unemployment was very low and, with good qualifications, the world was our oyster. Indeed, on the last day of the summer term 1970, with our results in our pockets, we headed up to London, only 16 minutes from Surbiton Station, all coming back with a job to start within a week or two. Most people were still paid weekly in cash and I only had to give a week's notice at Littlewoods. It felt very sophisticated therefore to open a bank account for my monthly salary to be paid into.

∞

I had landed a dream job and, even better, one of my college friends was going to be working in the same office.

Miki and I became the first in the new secretarial pool at Allardyce-Hampshire, a large advertising agency in Oxford Street in the centre of London's West End. It was a glamorous office, coincidentally, above the large Littlewoods store: two floors of modern offices filled with mostly young and trendy people. Office wear was very casual and my parents were horrified when I began to wear jeans and t-shirts to work. In the pool, we learnt the basics of the business and supported all the different Account Groups within the organization: a group consisted of an Account Director, an Art Director, a couple of Copywriters and a Secretary managing a number of clients. All except the Secretary would be men of course, although there were women in senior administrative positions such as Accounts and Personnel. It could be quite intense when deadlines were due and that was where the pool came in. As vacancies arose, we were offered positions within an Account Group and early in 1971 I was offered the post as secretary to the Brentford Nylons group. It was not the most glamorous client, indeed its nylon sheets were seen as distinctly common, being extremely uncomfortable and sweaty. However, the business which had started in 1959 was still largely successful and took out large double page advertisements in the weekend papers, then mostly broadsheet size. Each careful box, detailing every item of Brentford's range, had to be painstakingly cut out and pasted onto a huge template. It was the main form of advertising, although we sometimes paid for an advert on the fairly new independent television channel, ITN.

My Account Director was George. He was a round, little man with a huge temper and everyone in the company was rather afraid of him. I was not going to turn the job down but

I was secretly rather scared. However, I could stand up for myself and very soon found we got on rather well. I gained a reputation for dealing with difficult bosses! In contrast, our Art Director, Chris was a kind, gentle man and I loved working for him. He and Ron, one of the copywriters, managed the account, and George, very well and we became a close-knit group. This all changed when we were joined after a couple of years by Philip Yorke-Edgell, a rather flashy but glamorous young man. I am ashamed to say I was smitten, in a career sense and was persuaded by him to leave Allardyce and go to work for him when he set up his own agency in 1973. I lasted a month, he couldn't pay me and I very soon realized I had made a mistake.

But those years at Allardyce-Hampshire were wonderful. Working in central London, travelling up on the fast train from Surbiton with all the boys from youth club who had, by now, gained professional jobs, and living the London life. I had money in my pocket, a good job and lots of new friends. In addition to our salary, we received Luncheon Vouchers, 15p per day to buy lunch. This was strange currency to us, in February 1971 the UK had moved over from pounds, shillings and pence to the new decimal currency. 15p equated to 3 old shillings which was a generous amount. Many of the girls in our office would save vouchers for a week and then treat ourselves to lunch at one of the new Pizza restaurants opening up. I even had my first glass of red wine one Friday lunchtime! Many of the girls I met came from wealthy families in and around London and I began to be invited to house parties far afield. It became more and more difficult to abide by my mother's rules if I was travelling home after a party on the other side of London. My burgeoning social life also introduced me to many people from different backgrounds. Although the girls at school had been from all walks of life, I had not been to many of their houses. Now I was mixing with girls who had all the advantages of life. In the early 1970s attitudes towards women were still quite old-fashioned and many of the girls I met who became secretaries only expected to work for a couple of years before getting married and having a family. Their main aim in life was to have a good time – and why not? Young women had money in their pockets, there was full employment and wages were rising.

The economic situation seemed good for us, but for the country it was a different story. The 1960s had seen a rise in living standards and people were becoming more affluent. By the early 1970s wages had risen dramatically but not all workers had enjoyed the same increase in their income. On 9th January 1972, the National Union of Mineworkers called their members out on strike for the first time in 50 years. They were demanding a 36% increase on their pay, the government offered them 7.9%. This might seem a ridiculous request but their wages had fallen well below the average. On 16th February, the Central Electricity Generating Board announced that there would be nine hours of power cuts every day to save fuel. This did not just apply to households but to businesses and factories too, and the shift system put in place caused huge disruption to the economic life of the nation. At Allardyce, we dusted down the old manual typewriters (we were all using the modern electric typewriters in London), stuck candles to them and continued to work, whilst on the other side of Oxford Street the lights were still blazing.

1972 was a difficult year for the country in other ways. Following the 'Bloody Sunday' events in Northern Ireland, when fourteen protestors were killed by British troops, the IRA (Irish Republican Army) took revenge by bombing the Aldershot Barracks, killing 9 and injuring 19. The 'Troubles' as they were known started in 1969 and, although a ceasefire was called after the Aldershot bombing, the IRA continued to plant bombs over the next 20 years or more, finally coming to an end with the Good Friday Agreement brokered by Labour Prime Minister, Tony Blair, in 1998. In 1974 a pub in Guildford was bombed, it being popular with soldiers from the nearby Pirbright barracks. It was very close to home.

It was not a good summer for weather either, being wet and cool for much of the time. But for Matthew and I, it didn't dampen our ardour. Our relationship had developed quickly and we spent as much time together as we could. He was a trainee Quantity Surveyor and on a construction site to build the new YMCA in Tottenham Court Road, at the far end of Oxford Street. We often met after work and spent time together before getting the train home from Waterloo to our different stations. This caused trouble at home too, I did not want to say when I would be home or promise to be in for dinner but that was not acceptable. The traditional way was to go home from work, get dressed up and then go 'walking out' – my life just wasn't like that. We often did go out in the evenings of course, mainly at the weekends and I began to feel, for the first time that I had a real ally. We agreed on so much and discussed everything from books to politics but laughed a great deal too. Within a few months, we knew we would stay together.

I was very grateful for Matthew's support when I left Philip Yorke-Edgell and, given that we were seeing each other more and more, it made sense to me to leave the London lights and get a local job. So began my happy years at Gordon Simmons Research Agency. In early 1973, I answered an advertisement from one, Joan Macfarlane Smith, a rather eccentric lady starting up her own fieldwork agency. Market Research was a growing industry, the need to gather information about customers' needs and preferences to inform the burgeoning advertising industry was ever more important. It was a short step from advertising and a great chance to help form this exciting new company based in the offices of a quirky folly-like building, Ruxley Towers in Claygate. As Joan's Personal Assistant, I was instrumental in every part of the business and eventually took over much of the administration side. It was my first taste of management and I learnt a few hard lessons! The young fieldwork managers, Diane, Roz & Colleen, became close friends and we had a lot of fun though we worked hard. They helped me through the tearful conversations with my mother over planning my wedding – despite the fact that I had left home, once we were planning a marriage, my mother was in charge all over again. Diane and I became very good friends and I would often stay at her flat after an evening at The Foley Arms, even after I was married. She would often ask whether Matthew minded and I knew he never did. We were so young and determined to continue each to have our own life and that has stood us in good stead ever since.

I stayed at Gordon Simmons until we bought our first house and moved down to Farnborough in Hampshire in early 1976. It was a wrench leaving them all but I had learnt so much, not least that I loved work and the challenges it brought. I have always loved the camaraderie of the workplace and missed it dreadfully when I left work to have children. Even in the early 1970s it was not common to continue working as a mother but at least we did not have to stop work when we married like our mother's generation. It was not common, however, for married couples to work in the same company and often, formally forbidden. My move to A. Monk & Company in the mid-1970s was a good one: a good job and local to home. As the Personal Assistant to the Managing Director, I didn't mix much with the other 'girls', it was a very different atmosphere from that of a London office and they were all much older. There were lots of great lads though, it being a construction company and lunchtimes were great fun: in the spring and summer we would be on the putting green on the front lawn of our old house turned office in the autumn and winter we would have a card school playing Canasta. We had summer socials to which our partners were invited and it was there, in the summer of 1978, that my boss Dick Whittle offered my husband a job – only because I was due to leave to have our first child in a couple of months! There was no question of going back to work for me.

Notes:

1 Independent Television Network

Chapter Eleven
She's Leaving Home, Bye Bye

So, the time has come. I am leaving home to share a flat with my friend Vicki. She has a flat above a shop in Surbiton and needs a flat mate to share the rent. I am so lucky it came up because I have no choice really. Mum has discovered I am on 'the Pill' and is furious with me. It is the last straw. I cannot believe she has been searching my bedroom. She cannot believe I will no longer do as she says. Being with Matthew has given me more courage to stand up to her and, although she seems to like him, she can't let go. The arguments are daily and unbearable for everyone.

∞

The Beatles song *She's Leaving Home* was on their 1967 album *Sergeant Pepper's Lonely Hearts Club Band* and its words seemed very relevant. During my troubled teenage years, I ran away from home on a regular basis. I wasn't gone long and sometimes my absence wasn't even noticed but I could not bear to stay in the house after one of our increasingly bitter arguments. While Mum and Dad were downstairs watching television, I would be in my bedroom doing homework and I would often pack a bag and say I was leaving. My poor sisters would beg me not to and I am ashamed now of my histrionics.

While I was still at school and college, I obviously could not leave and really had no intention of doing so. There was one memorable occasion, however, when I could bear it no longer. One winter evening, I left home and walked the 20 minutes to the Orton's house, home of my friends Ken and Heather. Despite my teenage crush on Ken and our up and down relationship, we had become good friends as I had with Heather. I had spent many afternoons at their house, often watching football and it had become a safe haven. Their mother was kind but I was rather scared of their father, a probation officer, who I had rarely met. That memorable evening, he took me into his office and talked to me for a long time, first of course getting me to telephone my parents to tell them where I was. He made me realize in the kindest possible way that leaving home was not the way to solve the problem, at least not yet and that I needed to try and talk to my parents and tell them what I was feeling. I know he spoke to my parents and I imagine they were embarrassed and probably angry. It did make a difference though and I think we tried to rub along after that.

It seemed to me then, and still does, that once I was working and paying a large share of my wages into the household, I should have more freedom to decide my comings and goings. I desperately wanted to share things with my mother but somehow could never do so without disapproval and argument. I still needed support and guidance but couldn't ask for it. My mother's relationship with her own mother had probably been similar. She was the youngest child of four and she had rebelled, leaving home at 18 to seek her fortune in London. We were repeating family history. Later, when I had my own daughter, I was terrified that I would repeat those mistakes and drive my daughter away. I was determined not to be my mother. Probably only my children know whether I have succeeded. I always felt the most important thing for both my children was to know that they were loved unconditionally and that they did not have to earn my love. I was proud of them, whatever their achievements.

There were good times of course. One bright day, soon after I was 18, Mum and I went out for one of our few jaunts together. She had learnt to drive in 1971, the same year as me, and we drove in her wonderful Standard 10 down to Rye in East Sussex. It was a sunny day and all was right with the world. She bought me a pair of black patent shoes with silver buckles and we laughed like sisters together. This was a different side to Mum but I saw it all too rarely.

The day my mother challenged me with my contraceptive pills in her hand is as clear to me now as it was then, nearly 50 years ago. The strange thing was that I don't think she knew why she was so angry. Although there was still an expectation that you would not have sex before marriage, in reality that was not the case, the changes of the 1960s were firmly embedded and young people were making their own decisions about their lives. I suspect she was secretly relieved that I was being sensible and I was, after all, 19 years old. In fact, she never told my father, even when Matthew and I shared a flat together before our marriage.

For me, it was the fact she had been through my bedroom and I felt totally out of control. It was that night that I decided I must leave and within days had agreed with Vicky that I would move in to the spare room of her flat in Surbiton. Little did I know that, once gone, I would not be welcome back in the family home except by appointment. I tried dropping in on the way to or from church but a message was relayed to me that it was 'inconvenient'.

For Matthew however, life had just got harder. His parents had been going through divorce and he was living with his father and brother in their family home in Sutton. I did not meet his mother for many months though she used to phone and chat to me on a Saturday morning when I was there at the weekends. She became a great source of strength to me then, and in the years to come and, when I sadly lost my own mother to cancer in the 1980s, she continued to be a calming voice on the end of the phone whenever I needed to vent the frustrations of marriage and motherhood. The family home in Egmont Road, Sutton was sold to divide the proceeds and Matthew was to go and live with his mother in her new house in Banstead. There were a few weeks between the sale of one and the purchase of the other so Matthew became temporarily homeless – and moved in with me!

We had talked about marriage but had never intended to marry until Matthew was qualified. His Quantity Surveying course was three years and, of course in the same situation, most of our friends were still living at home and saving for their first house. That was not an option for us. I was paying rent and, having spent a few weeks together, we decided we wanted to live together, even though this was almost unheard of and certainly not approved of. We were young and in love and the chance of owning a house was a far-off dream.

So, in late 1972 we set a wedding date and moved into our flat in Cranes Drive. It was a lovely old house in Surbiton which had been converted into six flats, three on each floor. We had two rooms: a kitchen/diner and a bedroom/sitting room. We shared a bathroom with the two other flats on our landing. It seems incredible now but we were in heaven – we had our freedom and we had each other.

∞

The sun is shining, it is almost unbearably hot – the hottest day of this year, 1973. My long white Victorian-style dress is long-sleeved and high necked and I will roast. Dad and I are in the wedding car on our way to the church and he is gripping my hand very tightly. *"Be happy my love,"* says my father and I am sure there are tears in his eyes. I realize at that moment that we have grown apart. He has tried to keep the peace but it has been an uphill struggle. I suspect life is much happier for them all since I left home last year and I am nostalgic for that happy childhood relationship we had.

We are getting married at Surbiton Hill Methodist Church and the Rev. Harry Johnson will marry us. He has been our minister for some years so I know him very well. They are still my second family and I will carry on going there and helping with the Sunday School for years to come.

But a new life beckons. Matty and I are moving together into a bigger flat in Epsom. We will have the upstairs of an old house and our landlady lives downstairs. She is the Great Aunt of our best man, Rob Hackman, and we are very lucky to get it. It is an unfurnished flat which means we can make it ours and of course the rent is cheaper so we will start saving to buy our own house. That means a great deal to us but it will take time. Meanwhile, we are enjoying life. We have good jobs, lots of friends, and many plans for the future.

But that's another story …

∞

Wedding

Chapter Twelve
A Changing World

In 1953, the year of my birth and of the coronation of Queen Elizabeth II, Great Britain was already changing. After years of war and rationing, prospects looked bright. An awareness that a better society needed to be built had resulted in the introduction of the Welfare State to take care of the British people 'from the cradle to the grave'. This included free secondary education for all children until the age of 15, the formation of the NHS resulting in free health care for all and a National Insurance scheme to help people with unemployment, sickness and an old age pension. An Englishman, Edmund Hillary, had become the first man, with Sherpa Tensing, to scale the summit of Mount Everest. Britain was proud of itself.

That same year, petrol became unrationed for the first time since the war and huge numbers of cars (without seat belts) took to the roads. Quiet country roads became very busy and by the end of the decade a new word had entered the dictionary – motorways. To children's delight, though perhaps not good in the long run, sweets too became unrationed.

Clothes too changed dramatically. With fabric unrationed, dresses became fuller and young women threw off the rigid corsets needed by the 1940s fashions. Shrugging off the flat shoes worn during wartime and austerity, women started wearing high heels and glamour was everywhere. Men always wore a jacket, shirt and tie or perhaps a cravat, even to the pub.

However, many attitudes had not changed. Britain still had the death penalty for murder, homosexuality was illegal and women were still expected to carry out all the housework and child care and give up their careers on marriage.

The Royal Family were as formal and traditional as they had been throughout the century. Although the Queen and Prince Philip were regularly seen carrying out royal duties, their private lives were just that. There were few photos of the royal children and the press was respectful and non-interfering. Formal photographs and glimpses of the royals at events such as Ascot were all the British public could expect. This all changed in 1969 when a documentary about the Royal Family, compiled over 18 months of their public and private lives, kicked off the intense scrutiny the royals now receive from the public and the press. The film was withdrawn and has not been shown since. Princess Anne came to be a very modern royal, having a successful equestrian career, winning gold and silver European Championship medals and representing Great Britain at the 1976 Olympics. On her marriage to Captain Mark Philips, he refused a title and their children subsequently were born without titles. Anne wanted them to have as normal a life as possible. After 1958 young women were no longer presented at Court as debutantes, marking their entry into society.

The 1960s was a decade of huge change in the country. Shifts in law, politics and the media reflected a new individualism and a growing appetite to live in a more liberal society. People were becoming more affluent and had money in their pockets to spend on luxuries and even holidays abroad. They were less willing to conform and be told how to run their lives. Women began to go out to work after marriage and began to demand equality in their pay and conditions. Post-war immigration along with rapid social and technological change led to changes in attitudes but also to uncertainty about British identity.

Culture too was changing. The deferential attitudes of the working classes were disappearing and satire entered the mainstream. As more and more families had a television set, people began to see what others owned and learnt to question more about their lives. They began to stand up for their rights, both civil and at work. In 1960, Penguin won a not guilty verdict against the Crown, which had brought an obscenity prosecution against D.H. Lawrence's novel *Lady Chatterley's Lover*. First published in Europe in 1928, it was banned in Great Britain until the success of its case.

There were two momentous milestones for women. In 1961, the contraceptive pill became available on the NHS and in 1967 the Abortion Act was passed. There were laws affecting prostitution and divorce. Until the Divorce Reform Act 1969, unhappy couples would arrange for one spouse to book into a hotel to commit the adultery necessary for them to divorce. There was no such thing as breakdown of the marriage in the eyes of the law or, for that matter, the church.

The church's role in society was slowly diminishing. With the advent of shorter working hours (in 1952 the average worker worked a 48-hour week), people had more leisure time and there were many ways to spend it. Bowling alleys arrived in the UK in 1960 and quickly became a craze with young people. Coffee bars were opening up and Americanization was feared by the older generations. Recreational drugs became available and 'hippies' began to preach peace and freedom. For these young people, the church represented the old ways and it was seen as perpetuating the strict class-ridden society they wanted to be rid of.

The Profumo affair in 1963 scandalized the nation and forever changed the relationship between politicians and the press as well as seriously undermining the public trust in politicians which continues to this day. Many laws passed in the 1960s allowed women more freedom and feminism became a more influential ideology. More jobs became available to them and this allowed them to move away from home and become independent. With the advent of the contraceptive pill they were able to broaden their hopes and dreams beyond marriage and motherhood. The women workers' strike at Ford of Dagenham in 1968 led to the passing of the Equal Pay Act of 1970. Women were becoming increasingly involved in politics and in the professions at the highest levels.

By the time I was married in 1973, the British economy was showing signs of strain. The admirable move to better rights for workers had led to strong trade unions and there were many battles to come between unions and government. But there is no doubt that, those born in the 1950s and growing up in the 1960s and early 70s enjoyed a golden age of opportunity, social mobility and optimism. We believed in the power of society and the state's obligations. We wanted to continue to build that better world that had been dreamt of by the post war generation. Perhaps we have in some ways. Many attitudes are simply not acceptable in 21st century Britain but there is still great inequality and much intolerance. There is still much to be done.